ANXIETY CAN BE YOUR SUPERPOWER

ANXIETY
CAN BE YOUR
SUPERPOWER

MARK D. OGLETREE, PH.D.
& BRAYDEN MCFADDEN

CFI
An imprint of Cedar Fort, Inc.
Springville, Utah

© 2025 Mark D. Ogletree and Brayden McFadden
All rights reserved.

No part of this book may be reproduced in any form whatsoever, whether by graphic, visual, electronic, film, microfilm, tape recording, or any other means, without prior written permission of the publisher, except in the case of brief passages embodied in critical reviews and articles.

This material is neither made, provided, approved, nor endorsed by Intellectual Reserve, Inc. or The Church of Jesus Christ of Latter-day Saints. Any content or opinions expressed, implied or included in or with the material are solely those of the owner and not those of Intellectual Reserve, Inc. or The Church of Jesus Christ of Latter-day Saints." Permission for the use of sources, graphics, and photos is also solely the responsibility of the author.

Paperback ISBN 13: 978-1-4621-4942-1
eBook ISBN 13: 978-1-4621-4943-8

Published by CFI, an imprint of Cedar Fort, Inc.
2373 W. 700 S., Suite 100, Springville, UT 84663
Distributed by Cedar Fort, Inc., www.cedarfort.com

Library of Congress Cataloging Number: 2025931920

Cover design by Shawnda Craig
Cover design © 2025 Cedar Fort, Inc.

Printed in the United States of America
10 9 8 7 6 5 4 3 2 1
Printed on acid-free paper

CONTENTS

MARK'S STORY 1
BRAYDEN'S STORY 9

INTRODUCTION
Anxiety as a Superpower 17

SUPERPOWER 1
High Levels of Motivation... 25

SUPERPOWER 2
Empathy, Care, and Compassion 29

SUPERPOWER 3
The Spidey Sense.. 37

SUPERPOWER 4
An Analytical Mind 45

SUPERPOWER 5
A Nurturing Leader 55

SUPERPOWER 6
Self-Awareness 61

SUPERPOWER 7
Emergency Preparedness 71

SUPERPOWER 8
Being Healthy and Fit.. 81

SUPERPOWER 9
Resilience, Grit, and Moxie... 89

SUPERPOWER 10
Becoming Your Best Self 101

CONCLUSION
A Little Inconvenience 109

ENDNOTES 113
ABOUT THE AUTHORS 121

MARK'S STORY

Worry often gives a small thing a big shadow.
—SWEDISH PROVERB[1]

My story with anxiety began when I was three years old. My father died from the lingering effects of a car accident, and it rattled my world. When a three-year-old loses his father, he also loses his sense of stability and certainty. Shortly after my father's death, I began to bite my fingernails—a nervous habit to be sure, and one that I have maintained until the present day. In elementary school, I became aware that I was a worry wart mainly because my mom often called me that. Ironically, my mom is the biggest worrier I know.

Throughout my childhood and adolescence, I became more aware of my worries and fears. Although they did not impair me, I certainly kept them hidden from everyone else. I still remember an experience in fifth grade. I wasn't feeling well during class, and I walked to the front of the classroom and told Mr. Acker, "I don't feel very well." My next memory was of my teacher and several students huddled over me, putting smelling salt in front of my nose. I had passed out in front of the entire classroom. My mom came to the school and immediately took me to the doctor's office. After a quick assessment, the doctor said he couldn't find anything wrong with me and told my mom I had hyperventilated. He taught me how to breathe in a brown paper sack in case that happened again. Looking back on that experience, I'm sure my fainting spell had something to do with anxiety.

As I transitioned from adolescence to adulthood, I was aware that I was a worrier. I had fears that I didn't express to anyone—not even my wife. I managed to worry about almost everything—the economy, our financial problems, war, terrorism, failing out of graduate school, and worst of all, losing one of our children. However, I noticed that the busier I was, the smaller the space I had to worry. I think that is one of the reasons I enjoyed being in graduate school so much. I worked full time while I obtained two master's degrees and then a doctorate degree. While I was in school and working, there was little room for worry and fear. Once I finished school in my mid-thirties, I found plenty to worry about.

Here is a metaphor for the way I view anxiety. All of our fears, stressors, and worries are being constantly poured into a large cup. If we can manage those fears and concerns, we can keep the cup about one-half full of our challenges. However, if we are too busy to engage in some form of self-nurturing and choose to ignore our stresses and worries, eventually, the cup will overflow. This is what happened to me in my early forties.

The First Wave

One morning, I was looking up on a shelf in my walk-in closet for some sweatpants and realized the room was spinning. I had no idea what was happening, so I returned to bed, thinking I didn't get enough sleep. However, I was still dizzy thirty minutes later when I got out of bed, and the dizzy sensation remained with me for a few weeks, morphing into brain fog. Each day, I felt like I was on a heavy dose of cold medicine. The only hope that I found was that I usually felt fine after a good night's sleep. However, as the day wore on, the brain fog would set in, and I would spend most of my workday with this phenomenon. When I drove home from work at the end of the day, the fog would begin to lift, and I could enjoy a few hours of normalcy with my family before it was time to go to bed and repeat the same process the next day.

These symptoms caused me to visit several doctors. The first doctor, a family practitioner, wanted to simply treat me for vertigo by prescribing medicine. Unfortunately, the medicine only made me drowsy. I guess the treatment was to sleep through my dizziness. Second, I saw a neurologist, who recommended an MRI and wanted to test me for multiple sclerosis. Thankfully, he could find nothing wrong. Third, I visited a cardiologist who did a full work-up on my heart. Not surprisingly, he couldn't find anything wrong. I even visited an ear, nose, and throat specialist, and of course, he couldn't find anything wrong either. It was frustrating to live in this brain fog each day, and yet, not one medical professional could find anything wrong. I must have lived in this condition for a year or two. One day, my wife said, "Why don't you try a chiropractor? You have tried everything else, and nothing has worked." I thought, "Why not?"

The chiropractor seemed to have some answers. He believed my neck was misaligned and that a series of adjustments could help my brain be back to normal soon. Surprisingly, his treatment worked! Looking back on it now, I believe there was certainly a placebo effect— the chiropractor seemed to have answers, and his answers made sense. And, as a double bonus, I was feeling so much better. As he adjusted my spine and neck, my brain fog lifted! However, I realize now that the chiropractic treatment was only relaxing me. I would go to the chiropractor three times a week for several weeks, he they would massage my neck and back, and then he would do the adjustments. After a month of treatment, I felt better than ever. Did the chiropractic treatment really help, or was it the massage?

The Second Wave

My season of living without anxiety symptoms lasted for several years. It was wonderful! However, I was hit with a strong second wave, unlike anything I had previously experienced. By now, I was in my mid-forties. I retired from my job as an educator and was doing marriage and family therapy full time in my new practice. I was also the leader of my church congregation, which demanded many hours of my time. Furthermore, I was married to my wonderful wife, Janie, and we had eight busy children. We had five teenagers at the same time, and it was the most expensive time for our family, with children launching off to college, getting braces, driving, and participating in sports and music activities. Additionally, being self-employed for the first time caused some significant stress in my life. If I wasn't working in my office, we were not making any money. Vacations were stressful. First, I knew we were going to spend money, and second, while

I was out of the office, we would not make a dime! So, I took every counseling appointment I could. I saw more than forty clients a week, working every day, including Saturday mornings. I was at the church all day on Sunday, as well as two nights a week, in my role as a leader.

Looking back on these events, I can see that I was mega-stressed. One Saturday morning while I was visiting with a mother and her daughter in my counseling office, I began to experience a significant sensation like I had never felt before. I felt like I was dying. I had no control over my body, and I felt myself shutting down. Everything began to close in on me. It seemed like I was on the verge of passing out. A good friend of mine had died a few months before from a heart attack, and I felt like I was having my own cardiac episode.

I tried to compose myself. I wasn't sure what to say to my clients, but I finally admitted I wasn't feeling well and that I may vomit. That is a quick way to get people to clear a room! I abruptly ended our appointment so I could head to the restroom. My clients were kind and left quickly. I'm sure they assumed I had something contagious. I immediately called Janie and tried to explain what was happening. She tried to assure me that I had a flu bug. I tried to believe her—I wanted to believe her. But I felt this was much more serious, especially since I had never experienced this feeling before. I thought maybe I could gather myself and get my act together for my next appointment, which would have been twenty minutes later.

My next client came in, and I explained to him that I wasn't feeling well. I said I would try to power through our session but that we may have to reschedule. Sure enough, about ten minutes into our meeting, I began to experience the same sensation. I had no idea what was happening to me, but I felt I should get to a hospital quickly. I called Janie again, and this time we decided to call a friend, who was also a nurse, and get some counsel. She was unsettled enough to recommend that I go to a pharmacy and have my blood pressure checked. In those days, I didn't understand anything about blood pressure—I had no idea what those numbers meant. So, when I called the nurse back and gave her my blood pressure reading, she said, "Get to the emergency room immediately. You're going to have a stroke!" That got my attention.

My wife rushed me to our local hospital in Allen, Texas, and the doctors began to run some tests. Of course, they could find nothing wrong. Even my blood pressure that had been so high had come back down. Later, I was able to determine that I was having a panic attack and that the more I panicked, the more my blood pressure would spike. Nevertheless, at the time we didn't have any solid answers other than for me to go home and get some rest.

Unfortunately, over the course of the next few weeks, these symptoms continued. I felt like I was going to pass out. I was dizzy. I felt zapped of all energy and strength. I was jittery. I was hyper-alert and anxious. I felt cold—in fact, practically freezing. I had a hard time sleeping. I had no idea what was going on. I imagined that I was not going to live a long life because it was obvious that something drastic was wrong. During this time, there was a social event at our church. I remember walking in, and one of our dear friends saw me and said, "You look horrible." Although that was difficult to hear, I knew it was true. I was bothered that I could not conceal my problem as much as I thought I could.

One day, Janie came to my counseling office. We were going to go to lunch and figure out what to do with me. I had to take a phone call, so Janie sat in my office and began to thumb through some of my books. As she did so, she noticed a workbook that I used to help my anxious clients overcome their fears and worries. As she began to read, she became aware of the answer to my problem. When I hung up the phone, she said, "I know what your problem is."

I knew I had many problems, so I said, "Which one?"

She said, "Don't be silly, you know exactly what I am talking about!" She then read to me all of the symptoms of anxiety and panic from the workbook. I had every symptom! I was a textbook case for a person with generalized anxiety disorder and panic disorder. However, my pride kicked in. At that time, I owned my own private practice. I was a congregational leader. I was the father of eight children. I had a doctorate degree. I couldn't have anxiety—I treated people for anxiety! It took me some time to humble myself and admit that I did have anxiety.

Later I realized that I had an experience that had repeated several times long before I began to have these panic episodes. I would go through the same workbook Janie had picked up, reading the symptoms of generalized anxiety to one of my clients. As I read through those symptoms, I would quietly think to myself, "That is so funny. I have every one of these symptoms. It's a good thing that I do not have anxiety." Talk about denial.

Once we realized that I was dealing with anxiety, I felt a sense of relief that I did not have a serious medical problem. I got to work and started the exercises in the workbook that I used for my clients. I also had a good friend who was a therapist—we would often refer clients to each other. I asked him if I could have several visits to deal with my anxiety, and he graciously accommodated me. I also began to incorporate personal lifestyle changes, such as exercising more, eating healthier, losing weight, and getting more rest. I began to take days off work so I could have fun and enjoy my family. It worked! Life began to go well for several years, and then lightning struck for the third time.

The Third Wave

Janie and I had moved to Provo, Utah, where I had accepted a job as a professor at Brigham Young University. I was now in my late forties. Initially, I felt better physically than I had ever felt. The move from Texas to Utah would be a great way to push the "reset" button. However, moving to Utah and not being able to sell our Texas home (it was 2010 and the economy was horrible) was stressful. Moreover, I was also beginning a new job unlike any other I had ever had. We also moved from a place where we knew hundreds of people to somewhere where we knew very few. As I began my teaching career as a professor, I realized how stressful the life of a college professor can be if you are a task-oriented person like I am.

Within a week of the first semester, all of my anxiety symptoms returned with a vengeance. This time, I felt like I had to vomit each day. Sometimes I would go to a remote place on the campus where I could not be seen, hide behind a clump of trees, and vomit. I would compose myself, teach my classes, and then rinse and repeat the next day. I also felt so unsteady—practically wobbly—that I had to always hold on to the podium in our classroom for stability. This went on for several months. I knew that I had to get my life under control. I began to work on my problems again. I also received some therapeutic help. And this time, I decided that I would try medication. I couldn't believe when I walked out of Costco with my prescription for Zoloft that it cost only five dollars. I thought to myself, "I've been struggling with this anxiety for almost seven years now. If I take this pill and it works, I'm actually going to be so mad that the solution was this easy!"

The solution did work. I took the medication, and it helped immensely. I noticed that the anxious thoughts that plagued me almost daily subsided drastically. I was no longer dizzy or unstable. I wasn't cold, shaking, or nervous all day. And, since I was feeling so much better, I could exercise with greater intent and passion. I began to feel much better, and that trajectory continued. About six months later, I weaned myself off medicine and have never looked back.

I am now more than sixty years old. In many ways, my anxiety is behind me. I haven't had a panic attack or serious anxiety episode during the past ten years. Yes, occasionally I get overstressed, fearful, or nervous. However, I now have the tools necessary to combat my anxiety and live a healthy and normal life. I have enjoyed meeting with anxious clients and helping them by sharing with them what I have learned on my personal journey.

Along with Brayden, I look forward to sharing more of our anxiety experiences, some of the tools that have been helpful, and the ways anxiety can be viewed as a strength—even a superpower!

BRAYDEN'S STORY

Worrying is carrying tomorrows load with today's strength. . . . It is moving into tomorrow ahead of time.

—CORRIE TEN BOOM[2]

Prior to my first real experience with anxiety, one could say I had an idyllic life. Raised in a loving family in the suburbs of Texas, I was fortunate to have great experiences academically, religiously, socially, and athletically. I got into the university of my dreams and was blessed to play football there as well. As a freshman, I, like many other young men of my faith, submitted an application to serve a two-year ecclesiastical mission for our church. I soon learned that I would be spending the next two years of my life in Alaska doing missionary work. Consequently, the tail end of my freshman year of college was one of excitement, anticipation, and an overall feeling that I was on top of the world. Little did I know that my idyllic life was about to take a massive turn.

The First Wave

I spent the summer after my freshman year preparing to go to Alaska. When the time came, I entered the missionary training center with excitement and a little trepidation. I would spend the next two and a half weeks there preparing to go to Alaska for the next two years of my life. When it was my time to leave, I gave my family one last phone call and then excitedly boarded the plane to Alaska.

The second I got off the plane in Anchorage, I felt a shift in my brain. Thoughts of excitement and anticipation turned to realization and shock. It had not fully hit me that I would be in Alaska for the next two years of my life until I arrived there. I had been riding an emotional wave since I stepped into the missionary training center, and that wave came crashing down when reality set in. I remember sitting in our orientation meeting with the other missionaries and feeling as if a dark cloud had settled over my brain, muting the sights and sounds around me and filling my thoughts with thunderheads of worry and doubt. I assumed it was just me adjusting to the realities of missionary work, and I committed to push through it and work hard.

I was assigned a companion who I would live with, teach with, and learn from. We went to our apartment outside of Anchorage in the suburb of Eagle River and began our missionary work. I believed that as soon as I dove into the work and tried to do my best to care about others, my thoughts would unravel and the dark cloud I felt settle over me would dissipate. I had always been taught that when something didn't feel right, I could always work harder to rectify the problem. However, this seemed to have the opposite effect on my mental health. The dark cloud *did not* dissipate. There were times when the heaviness would lighten a little and I felt more like myself. However, that cloud always returned with a fury, and the maelstrom of powerful negative thoughts and worries would batter me relentlessly.

The best way I can describe it was that it felt like there were three individuals in my head. One was constantly freaking out, keeping up a constant dialogue of negativity and panic, continually high-strung and worried. The second individual was constantly trying to calm the first, trying to counterbalance the constant negativity and assure the first individual that we were safe and there was nothing to worry about. The final individual was the one who had to face the world and interact with others. This individual was aware of the constant battle between the other two. However, this facet of myself did not have the luxury of expressing this internal conflict; rather this part of me had to smile, laugh, and participate in conversations with the outside world.

This constant internal struggle essentially wrecked me. There were times when my panic would overwhelm my defenses and run rampant in my brain. My thoughts would spiral into increasingly horrific patterns that I felt I could not stop. It felt as if my mind was a runaway train that I had no ability to stop or hinder. When these moments occurred, I would become very quiet and subdued. My head would feel hot, and my eyes would glaze over as I focused on the hopeless task of restraining my runaway brain. I found that getting up and moving around helped, but there were times when we were in meetings or otherwise engaged and I would just have to bear the brunt of the panic without being able to move. I stopped eating, as all my energy went to fighting this internal battle. My once affable and outgoing personality changed to one of silence and seriousness. I began to lose weight, and my athletic body turned into a shadow of itself. It became hard for me to maintain eye contact, and my once proud shoulders began to slump under the constant weight of my own thoughts.

It is important to note that at this time, I had no idea I was dealing with anxiety and panic attacks. I had never dealt with them before. My companion also had no real education on anxiety either. We both felt as if I was experiencing a major adjustment to missionary life and that I just needed to keep working my hardest to get through it. Every night I would pray for a miracle. I hoped that the next morning I would wake up with a sound mind, ready to attack the day. To the contrary, each morning I would wake up with an impending sense of dread, and my mind would waste no time in assailing me with its mental barrage of negative and panic-inducing thoughts. I felt as if the pain was too much. Although my family was always a great support to me, I did not mention the extent of my struggles to my parents in my weekly emails. I am the oldest of five children, and I was trying to set a good example for my siblings. I felt that the only way I could do that was to power through these mental adversities and come out the victor.

Week by week, my mental fortitude grew weaker and weaker. Eventually, I was having four massive panic attacks a day. I could not sleep well. Every time I would awake in the night, my mind would instantly start its assault again, and I would not be able to go back to sleep. Despite this inability to sleep, evenings were my favorite time of day because I knew that I was going to bed soon and I could get a fleeting reprieve from the onslaught that assailed me constantly. My thoughts became darker and darker, and I began to think of ways I could hurt myself to be able to be sent home. It wasn't as if I was being forced to stay in Alaska against my will. It was genuinely my fault because I was too stubborn to admit how hard things were for me, and I was too prideful to reach out for the mental health help I desperately needed. Hence, I often thought of some twisted ideas and elaborate methods to get me sent home. I thought of breaking my own ankle, stealing the car and driving to Anchorage and booking a ticket for the next flight home, and, scariest of all, ending my own life.

This particularly dark thought came to me one evening as I was lying on my back in our apartment. I had just had a panic attack, and my body and mind were exhausted from the struggle. I remember sluggishly looking over and seeing the cord from our fan laying on the ground next to me. I thought of how easy it would be to wrap that cord around my neck and end it all. The scariest part was how appealing this thought seemed to feel as I lay there. The next day I looked back on that memory and became very scared at how easy it was for me to contemplate such a terrible way to end my life. Once I realized that committing suicide had become acceptable, I was shocked out of my own pride and stubbornness. I decided it was time to come clean and let my parents know of the full extent of my mental suffering.

I reached out to my parents, and they contacted my mission president, who I met with that very day. I was sent to a Church psychologist who interviewed me and had me take a mental health test. I remember seeing the psychologist's eyes grow wider and wider as he looked at the test results. I thought to myself, "Well, Brayden, that is one test you did not want to ace."

After my appointment, my mission president called and said I would be on the next flight back home to Texas. Part of me was relieved, while another part of me was ashamed that I had given up. I spent the whole plane ride home doing anything I could to distract myself from how embarrassed I was of myself and the abject failure I perceived that I had become.

Upon my arrival in Texas, I deboarded the plane and walked to the baggage claim. There was no one to greet me, and I sat alone as I waited for my luggage. As it turns out, my parents were sent to the wrong baggage claim, so they arrived a few minutes after I did. When they called out to me and I turned to them, my mom instantly burst into tears and grabbed me. My mom is not one to cry in public, so later, when I asked her why she cried so hard when she saw me, she told me that when she saw me, it was like seeing a shadow of her son. The proud, confident young man she had said goodbye to a couple of months earlier was gone. In his place was a hollow-eyed youth who looked as if he carried the weight of the world on his shoulders, dressed in a suit that looked way too big on him.

On the ride home, I sat in the back seat and cried while my mom sat next to me and held my hand. I remember mumbling, "I'm sorry," and, "I failed," over and over again through my tears while my mom and dad reassured me that I was not a failure and that I was very brave for doing what I did. When we arrived home, I received nothing but love from my siblings, and my mind began to relax as I settled into my childhood home. I went upstairs to our media room to take a nap, feeling content that the worst of it was over for me. To my surprise, I had a panic attack a short time later. This was the first sign that I had brought the dark cloud home with me.

Over the next couple months, I was in and out of doctors' offices as they searched for ways to help me. Therapists, neurologists, psychologists, and massage therapists all took a crack at treating me. Over the course of these visits, I learned about anxiety and what it does to the brain and body. I took a variety of medications as the professionals attempted to find one that would help. Despite their best efforts, the dark cloud persisted. Neurologists told me I could no longer play football. That psychological blow did not help my already dark outlook on life. I began to lose my faith as well, not wanting to believe in a higher being that would allow these kinds of things to happen to me while I was only trying to serve others.

Depression soon followed the anxiety, and I fell deeper and deeper into a mental pit. Over the span of a couple months, I had gone from a division one college football player to someone who couldn't even get out of bed and take a shower without help from his parents. I finally got to a point where I wanted to renounce my faith, renounce everything that made me who I was, and just give up on trying to ever feel better and consign myself to a life of mental misery.

A conversation with my mom changed everything. She told me that she would love me no matter what I choose to do with my life, but that I needed to decide if everything I was and all I had become up to this point in my life was worth fighting for. After thinking long and hard about it, I decided that I could not give up on myself and that I needed to fight for a better tomorrow. With this reinforced will, I attacked my recovery. Change came slowly. We learned that I had suffered multiple concussions from my high school football days that had never been diagnosed. The trauma from these concussions were contributing to my anxiety and depression. This discovery helped us in our search for medication that would work well for me. I found a therapist who understood me and helped me so much that I decided to write this book with him. We found coping strategies that helped me reduce my general anxiety and helped me through panic attacks. I began to regain my faith, and the cloud over my mind began to dissipate.

This lifting of my anxiety was not the heavens parting and a rush of light coming into my life that I had hoped for. It was a gradual experience that could not be noticed day by day but rather month by month. I slowly healed and began to become myself again. This healing process was by no means quick, and it took quite some time before I would say I was back to 100 percent. But I did heal. I did grow. I did learn.

The Second Wave

Roughly three years after the traumatic events of my mission, I was back to being my former self. By this time, I was set to graduate from college and had many opportunities for work and graduate school. I was excited about the future and ready to take on the world. I accepted a position with the Department of Justice and prepared to head to California, where I would be working. By this time, I no longer took medicine and had not attended therapy because I felt like I was strong and whole again. The extensive background check I had to undertake for my job seemed to corroborate this sentiment and found me to be fully healthy and ready to go. Once I arrived in California, however, the old storm clouds made an appearance.

The all-too familiar fight against my brain began to ramp up again. The three individuals in my head returned in full force. Unfortunately, the panic attacks came back, along with the overthinking, spiraling thought processes. Once again, the affable, smiling, confident version of myself gave way to the quiet, brooding, painful reality of dealing with intense anxiety.

I couldn't believe it. I was reliving trauma I thought I had put behind me. Emotions I thought I had overcome returned with a vengeance. I tried once again to deal with my anxiety, but because of my own hubris, I could not utilize the skills I had learned the first time around due to a mistaken sense that I no longer needed them. I also had stopped taking the medication that had helped me so much during my first experience with extreme anxiety because, once again, I felt I no longer needed it.

The all-too familiar pattern began again. I could feel myself slipping back into that dark, terrible place I had been in a few short years before. This time, however, I reached out for help almost immediately. After days of consulting with my parents and my therapist, it was decided that I needed to relocate somewhere safe for me to stabilize and heal again. Once again, I packed up my things and headed back to the relative safety of a familiar place. The shame came back. The embarrassment came back. The feelings of mental fragility and weakness came back. The demons I thought I had dealt with proved all too eager to reenter my life and attempt to make up for lost time. Once again, I had gone from an individual capable of great things, an individual who had graduated from college with honors and begun a very promising career, to someone who could not get out of bed for hours upon waking up because the mental torment was too much.

Thankfully, I did not stay in this state for long. Once again, I pulled myself up and did the things necessary to heal. I began taking my medication again. I returned to therapy, where I was able to address issues that I had not addressed initially. This allowed me to go from "good enough to function" to "living life to the fullest." I learned more about myself and how my own particular anxiety works. I held onto my faith instead of abandoning it, using it as support when days became too difficult instead of a scapegoat for why these things kept happening to me. I was open with my parents and allowed them to help me and support me when I wasn't able to do so myself. Utilizing all of these tools, I began to change into a better version of myself. I changed so much that my perspective on anxiety began to change. I began to see my anxiety not as a weakness but as a strength. I saw how it motivated me even as it was bringing me down. I saw how it helped me, even in the depth of my pain, get a job in the industry that I truly care about and have a passion for. I saw how it helped increase my empathy toward others in a manner that allowed me to comfort them as few others could. I saw how it fueled my goals and aspirations. I saw how what I had perceived as my greatest weakness became one of my greatest strengths.

I begin this book with my personal anxiety journey for a reason. I want you to see that I get it. I have been there. Anxiety is not just something I have researched and learned about from books; it is something I have experienced. Moreover, not only have I experienced anxiety, but I have also experienced some of the worst symptoms that can psychically damage a person mentally, physically, and spiritually. And even with this background, I still can confidently say that I see anxiety as a strength, not a weakness. The modern world wants us to see anxiety as a disease that is to be managed and minimized. All anyone wants to talk about is how to cope with their anxiety or how to overcome it.

That is not what I am here to tell you. I am here to tell you that you can thrive with anxiety. Along with Mark, I would even go so far as to say that anxiety can be a superpower.

INTRODUCTION

Anxiety as a Superpower

*Trust yourself. You've survived a lot,
And you'll survive whatever is coming.*

—*Robert Tew*[3]

Anxiety* *can't* be a superpower. How can something that is classified as a mental health problem be considered a good thing? How can a condition that requires some individuals to take medicine, others to need life-long therapy, and even others to be hospitalized be considered a superpower? Are we crazy for even suggesting such a concept?

Viewing anxiety as a superpower might be out of the ordinary, but that is precisely why this perspective is so important. The world looks at anxiety through the lens created by the previously stated questions. Worldly parameters and ideologies have chosen to focus on the negative aspects of anxiety. We call this viewing anxiety from a "deficit" perspective. In fact, this is the outlook I had on anxiety when I was first diagnosed. I saw it as a burden; something that I would have to "deal with" for the rest of my life. I followed along with the widely accepted perception that an anxiety diagnosis equaled a change in my life that I would need to constantly work at to manage.

More and more people are being forced to face this mental adjustment. When COVID-19 first impacted the globe, a scientific brief released by the World Health Organization stated that in the first year of the pandemic, anxiety and depression increased globally

---

*   This chapter was written by Brayden McFadden.

by 25 percent. This rise in anxiety and depression levels especially impacted young adults, with up to 48 percent reporting mental health symptoms. While numbers have gone down since the initial onset of the pandemic, compromised mental health remains a key issue impacting many demographics of modern society.

This is why we care so much about changing the perception around anxiety. With an increasing number of people being exposed to anxiety, there are so many who, just like me, received their diagnosis and immediately made the mental leap of trying to determine how they were going to "live with" or "deal with" this new aspect of their life. In the following sections I will give a brief overview of my own change from seeing anxiety as a hindrance to seeing it as a superpower. I will also discuss the reasons anxiety can be a superpower, a topic that will be discussed in the remaining chapters.

From Sullen to Superpower

I distinctly remember the appointment where I was diagnosed with anxiety. It was my first doctor's appointment since returning from my mission, and my father had come with me for support. As the doctor told me about the anxiety and what to expect, I sat in a large, comfortable armchair and looked out the window onto a parking lot. I wanted to deny what I was hearing; in fact, I wanted to say that I was fine and just needed some rest and recuperation. Ironically, as I was considering this new possibility, I was fighting off a panic attack that threatened to engulf me right there in the doctor's office.

And so began my life with anxiety. For years after that appointment, I saw my anxiety exactly as the world prescribed it; something that I needed to work at to limit and lower the impact it might have on living a "normal" life. However, as I came to understand my anxiety more, I began to see that not everything concerning anxiety had to be doom and gloom. I saw in little tidbits how anxiety made me stand out from my peers in different, positive ways. I saw the increased levels of empathy that anxiety could provide, the extra motivation to get a project done, or the self-awareness to understand what I needed as a unique individual. These realizations came in brief flashes that I did not string together until my second wave with major anxiety.

As I mentioned before, the second wave hit when I was in California at my first job out of college. When I left California and began to heal from that second wave of anxiety, I truly began to understand how anxiety could benefit me. I learned the power of self-talk from my therapist, and it felt like this was a crucial piece of the puzzle that I had been missing when it came to understanding my anxiety. With this important piece in place, I used my expanded toolkit of strategies to address my anxiety, and I began to thrive. As I saw all of the good that came from understanding my anxiety and addressing it, I thought, "Could anxiety really be as bad as some people seem to think?" This was a revolutionary thought for me. Until then, I had only considered it a horrible illness. To even think it might have some actual benefit seemed insane. And then I thought of all of those little moments of clarity over the years where I had seen how anxiety could benefit me and everything finally recalibrated in my brain.

Assuming that I might have just cracked and gone crazy, I began researching online to see if anyone successful dealt with anxiety. To my amazement, the list was long. I saw names such as Beethoven, Van Gogh, Abraham Lincoln, Winston Churchill, Ryan Reynolds, and Selena Gomez. It dawned on me that anxiety could be a double-edged sword; you could either be severely limited by it or utilize it to become an extremely high-functioning individual. I tested this new mindset by asking people I knew were anxious how they saw it as a benefit in their lives. The question often took them off guard, but after a little introspection, they always replied with something like, "You know, now that you mention it, anxiety has helped me to have a desire to set goals and work hard to achieve them." More specifically, some said their anxiety motivated them to get good grades in school or to have a drive and passion to practice harder in sports. Not once did they fail to mention how anxiety made their life different, but each person also recognized how anxiety had been a blessing to them.

As this mindset gained more and more traction in my head, I decided I would take it to Dr. Mark Ogletree, who was not only my therapist and friend from home but also a distinguished professor at Brigham Young University. I was filled with trepidation when I began to outline this idea of anxiety being a benefit because I thought it might just be a silly thought experiment that would have no merit in the eyes of a professional. To my surprise, Mark not only agreed with me but said that he, too, believed anxiety could be a benefit to an individual. Now armed with the knowledge that this mindset had merit, I further elaborated that anxiety could be kind of like a superpower; something that, if properly understood and controlled, could propel a person to heights beyond which they could not have normally achieved. Mark loved the idea, and we set out to see if there was anyone else in the professional/academic realm with a similar opinion.

While we found many individuals who agreed with our assessment, we found that few people, if any, had attempted to write extensively about how anxiety could be a benefit and not only a hindrance. After reviewing the research, we felt that we needed to add our ideas of anxiety being a superpower into the existing literature on anxiety. Using our own personal experiences, coupled with established facts, we came up with ten basic ways that anxiety can be seen as a superpower. Consider the following suggestions, or attributes, that can allow our anxiety to actually bless us, rather than hinder us.

1. High Levels of Motivation

Anxious individuals' brains often will not stop going no matter the time of day. From the second I wake up to the second I go to sleep, I am thinking about the tasks I need to get done that day. In fact, I am often thinking of all of the assignments and responsibilities I need to address for the entire week, as well as many other things. This high mental motor can translate to a high physical motor. I have a hard time sitting around when I know there are things I could be doing. This results in a highly motivated mentality that helps me accomplish tasks at a higher rate than the average individual.

2. Empathy, Care, and Concern

Newton's third law of motion states: For every action there is an equal and opposite reaction. People who have anxiety often spend a lot of time in their own head, usually dealing with a high-strung brain that likes to explore every negative scenario in life and all of the negative facets of our own mental image. Because of this, like Newton's law states, people with anxiety have a greater ability to understand and empathize with a wide range of situations and emotions outside of themselves. I have often seen someone with the far-off look in their eye that I get when I'm struggling with a particularly hard emotion or situation. I instantly understand what that situation feels like and am able to feel empathy for that person.

3. The Spidey Sense

Have you ever gone to a social event and felt like you needed to analyze and categorize every single face you see? Have you ever gone to a restaurant and wanted to sit in a corner booth because you wanted to be able to see the rest of the restaurant so nothing would surprise you? Having an anxious brain can cause you to always be on the alert. Because anxiety can make us high strung, we often want to be able to have some form of control over every situation we are in. This results in a hyper-awareness that is often lost on people that do not have anxiety. Such a hyper-awareness and high level of sensitivity allows people with anxiety to pick up on things quicker than others and be able to maintain a level of situational awareness that can be seen as a version of Spider-Man's spidey sense.

4. An Analytical Mind

Anxiety can further develop an already analytical mind or help someone who is not analytical become so. In order to understand our anxiety better, we need to understand ourselves. Examples include figuring out how our anxiety reacts to certain stimuli or discovering coping methods that limit the more pronounced effects of anxiety. All these internal tests and studies result in an analytical framework being necessary to maximize our understanding of how our brain and anxiety coexist. The analytical methodology we apply to understand our anxiety can be extrapolated and applied to many other things in life. I have used my analytical mind to effectively study for tests, achieve success at work, and become a better friend and family member.

5. A Nurturing Leader

Much like the highly motivated facet addressed above, the high motor brain that is common to people with anxiety can also help develop these individuals into leaders. Because people with anxiety like to achieve and accomplish, and can become more stressed if things they know should be getting done are not, they can be a catalyzing factor in any group they are a part of. This usually means that such individuals thrive in leadership roles. Ironically, I feel less anxiety when I am in charge of a project or group because I know that I can have a driving factor in completing the assignment. Many of the benefits of anxiety line up well with factors that make a good leader. However, those will be expounded upon further in the chapter covering leadership potential.

6. Self-Awareness

Socrates once said, "To know thyself is the beginning of wisdom." People with anxiety are some of the most self-aware people in the world. Because we spend so much time in our own heads, we come to know that space pretty well. When I was first learning about my anxiety, I engaged in much introspection and self-study to understand how my anxiety works within the framework of my head. During this self-study, I not only learned about my anxiety triggers and relievers but also about my limits and how to tell when I was approaching them. The introspection has continued, and I have come to understand my headspace well and feel as if I know myself on a level I never could have imagined.

7. Emergency Preparedness

Earlier I mentioned that people with anxiety like to think about any and every potential situation and how it might impact them. This translates into them being pretty good doomsday preppers of sorts. One of my biggest triggers—and certainly one I see in many other people filled with anxiety—is the fear of losing control. This could be in a mental, physical, or emotional context. Because of this, I try to prepare for every potential catastrophe so that I limit the chances of not being in control. This can manifest in different ways but usually results in people with anxiety being more prepared for emergency situations because if there is a potential for it, the anxious person has thought of it.

8. Being Healthy and Fit

This sometimes surprises people. Studies show that people who are more anxious and stressed tend to live shorter lives than those who have a more mellow outlook on life. The key principle here is the level of anxiety and stress. Just because we have anxiety doesn't mean we are anxious and stressed all the time; on the contrary, we are constantly trying to find ways to alleviate our anxiety and stress. Because so many proven stress and anxiety relievers involve some sort of fitness, people with anxiety can be better about maintaining a good fitness regimen as a counter to the more negative aspects of anxiety. This also translates to eating habits. Research has shown that avoiding certain foods and eating a healthy diet actually alleviate bad anxiety; therefore, people who deal with anxiety have extra motivation to maintain a relatively clean diet.

9. Resilience, Grit, and Moxie

It seems almost like an oxymoron to assume that people with anxiety can be more resilient than those who don't have anxiety. Due to our society's current view of anxiety, there is a stereotype that individuals with anxiety are one detrimental event away from going into a downward spiral. This perception of fragility is anything but true. People with anxiety are some of the most resilient people in the world because most of them have faced their fears and triggers. Knowing our limits and boundaries is not a lack of resilience; rather, it is the very definition of resilience because we are aware of how we can withstand difficult circumstances and have already established the necessary steps to recover quickly from difficulties.

10. Becoming Your Best Self

This final benefit is an amalgamation of all of the preceding ones. Because you are highly motivated, you will succeed when others cannot. Because you have empathy and care due to the mental tangles you have endured, you can help others. Because you are self-aware, you understand yourself and what you are capable of. In fact, there are myriad possibilities. Anxiety can take a lot out of you, but it can also help teach you how to become the best version of yourself.

Conclusion

We have discussed ten reasons we believe anxiety can be a superpower. Are you still not convinced? We invite you to join us on our journey through this book, where you will more clearly see how anxiety can actually benefit and bless your life.

Questions for Thought
1. What is your current outlook on anxiety?
2. How have you seen anxiety be a blessing rather than a burden?
3. Have you seen any of the above benefits manifest in your own life?

SUPERPOWER 1

High Levels of Motivation

Nothing diminishes anxiety faster than action.

—WALTER ANDERSON[4]

Did you know that 19 percent of Americans are affected by anxiety disorders each year? However, only 37 percent of those people receive treatment for anxiety.[5] Approximately 31 percent of adults in the United States will experience anxiety at some point in their lives.[6] Anxiety has now become more prevalent than depression in our country. Too many people have anxiety, and not enough are getting the help they need to overcome their worries and fears.

You may be surprised that many famous people have dealt with anxiety. Emma Stone, Michael Phelps, Ryan Reynolds,[7] Harrison Ford, Donny Osmond,[8] Abraham Lincoln, Franklin Roosevelt, Martin Luther King Jr., Winston Churchill,[9] Terry Bradshaw, and Steve Young all have struggled with anxiety at different points of their lives, but each are highly accomplished in their fields of expertise.

Anxiety and worry can be strong motivators. Often, those who have anxiety are people who get things done. In fact, performance anxiety is what drives people to accomplish so much in this life, and often in a short time period. In one study, higher levels of anxiety were associated with higher levels of effort and performance.[10]

Mark relays the following experience on how his anxiety was a motivator.

> My anxiety has propelled me to want to succeed and perform at a high level. I have accomplished more than I

ever dreamed, and I believe my anxiety can be blamed for that. For example, I was a below-average student in high school. It wasn't that I was dumb; I just didn't try. However, my high school academic counselor told me I should not consider college. She did not think I would have what it took to be a successful college student. Not only did my school counselor's recommendation cause me some anxiety, but I was also determined to prove her wrong. I went on to graduate from college with a respectable grade point average. After I finished my undergraduate degree, I went on to complete two master's degrees and a doctorate degree. I have also written numerous books and articles. I have presented papers at national and international conferences. I do not want this to sound arrogant, but much of my motivation came from a high school counselor who essentially said, "You'll never amount to much. You may as well just join the military and forget about going to college."

Often, those who have anxiety are overachievers—they want to be successful, they want to lead, and they often want to help others succeed. Both Mark and I are like this. Neither of us can sit still, and we certainly can't sleep in. We wake up early in the morning with many thoughts driving us to want to get out of bed and get going. Anxiety will not let us be spectators while the world passes us by. Those of us with anxiety feel a need to make a to-do list. With each item we check off, we feel accomplished. And the more we achieve in a given day, the calmer and more relaxed we can become. Therapist Kristine Tye wrote:

> Many people who have a form of anxiety are chronic overachievers. Anxiety is often used as a tool to help you push yourself to your limit of achievement. . . . The energy that fuels anxious thoughts and behaviors is giving you what you need to take action and get unstuck. By not taking action, the energy is just getting bottled up inside you with nowhere to go but in circles. . . . Taking action can channel

and alleviate that pressure, and the stress response can help you have the energy to do that.[11]

Indeed, worry and anxiety can be the fuel that drives us to achieve and accomplish our goals and dreams. Worry and fear can kick us out of bed each morning and propel us to tackle the day.

Not All Anxiety Is Debilitating

We know that anxiety is associated with restlessness, irritability, fatigue, difficulty concentrating, and disturbed sleep. Some experts have even associated worry with poor health outcomes, damaged relationships, and low self-worth. But worry and fear can be motivational. Worry can serve as a catalyst for analytical thinking and planning.[12] Other researchers have shown that anxiety can facilitate problem-solving.[13]

Think about it. If you are worried or anxious about getting in a car wreck, you may be more likely to drive more cautiously or wear a seat belt. If you are worried about your health, you may be more likely to exercise and eat cleaner. If you are worried about skin cancer, you will most likely wear sunblock.[14] If you are worried that you may fail an upcoming exam, you are more likely to study more seriously. Overall, our anxiety can motivate us to put more time, effort, and energy toward a cause.

Another aspect of worry and motivation is that if there is a stressor in our lives that causes concern, it often stays in the forefront of our minds until we do something about it.[15] Mark gives the following example from his experience with clients.

> I often tell my clients in my practice that one of the greatest treatments for anxiety is solving the problem that is causing you to worry! If your knee hurts, quit whining about it to your significant other. Go to the doctor and get your knee checked out. Perhaps you will find that there is nothing to worry about—at least for now. If you are always wringing your hands over your finances, then go home and create a budget, get another job on the side to help increase your

income, or meet with a financial planner to determine what your course of action should be. Go solve your problem!

Another aspect of worry or anxiety is that the consequences of our anxiety are often so unpleasant, we will find ways to reduce our worries and fears.[16] We can become proactive in our coping responses or take action steps that will lead us to a solution. Worry can inspire individuals to resolve conflict, plan ahead, and act. "In sum, just as fear motivates escape and anger motivates retaliation, worry motivates preparation and prevention. When people have control over a future outcome, worry illuminates the importance of taking action to prevent an undesirable outcome and keeps the situation at the front of one's mind to ensure that appropriate action is taken."[17]

Conclusion

If you have anxiety and your life is filled with worry, take heart. Many of us have anxiety. But instead of allowing your anxiety to take over your life, own your anxiety. Embrace it! Convert your anxiety into a superpower. Leverage your anxiety to motivate you instead of paralyze you. Anxiety and worry can be a motivator to accomplish more than you ever dreamed.

Questions for Thought

1. As you look back on your life, can you recognize times when worry and fear motivated you to achieve something?
2. How can you use your own anxiety as a motivator to be successful?
3. Have you ever thought to look at your anxiety as a motivator and not a hindrance?

SUPERPOWER 2

Empathy, Care, and Compassion

Fear is conquered by action. When we challenge our fears, we defeat them. . . .When we dare to face the things which scare us, we open the door to freedom.

—AUTHOR UNKNOWN

It's true that anxious people share similar personality traits that contribute to their anxiety. For example, often, these people are analytical worriers who tend to think more deeply about things than others. Moreover, such individuals often have high expectations for themselves and others. Sometimes, they can even be perfectionistic in certain aspects of their lives. Anxious people often seek the approval of others, and they hope that everyone will like them. These individuals also like to be in control of their lives—they want life to be predictable.[18]

But remember, despite these traits, anxiety can be your superpower. Lucinda Bassett, nationally renowned motivational speaker and life coach, wrote to those who have anxiety:

> Here's the good news: you're special. If you are someone who experiences more than the average amount of anxiety, you are full of potential and greatness. Why? Because you probably have above average intelligence. You are highly creative with a fabulous imagination. You are detail-oriented and analytical. These are wonderful traits that can make you extremely successful and enable you to accomplish great things. Unfortunately, people with anxiety disorders

tend to use their attributes to scare themselves. They over intellectualize, overanalyze, and use their creativity to envision the worst possible scenarios. Used in a negative way, our wonderful traits can make us sick.[19]

Isn't it great to know that those who are anxious have above-average intelligence, are highly creative, have a healthy imagination, and are detailed oriented and analytical? These are the attributes of strong members of society, and certainly strong leaders. There are many positive attributes associated with those who have anxiety. Here is another common personality trait shared by the anxious: they tend to be kind, caring, compassionate, and sensitive to the needs of others.

The anxious person cares about others. They often exercise charity and benevolence because they are in tune with the needs of those around them. They know when others are hurting or need love and attention.

The anxious person is truly empathetic. They often feel what others are feeling. Mark shared the following reflection:

> I used to watch the news at night before bed. I would often be disturbed as I viewed stories about murder, kidnapping, fires, death, disease, and natural disasters. Sometimes, I would specifically think, "I wonder how that father is doing tonight, now that his house burned down," or, "How does that mother feel, whose child just drowned in a back yard pool?" I found myself overly worried for those who had experienced tragedy or heartache. I was also aware that not everyone thought this way.
>
> When smaller tragedies happened at a more localized level, like in our neighborhood, or among members of our church congregation, I would often feel compelled to visit those families, send them a card, or bring them some food. The good news is that such sensitivity inspired me to act often.

Many of those who experience anxiety have a built-in radar that can detect those around them who are struggling. In some ways, it is like a sixth sense. In fact, we know of a woman who grew up in our hometown in Texas who seemed to have this trait. Wherever she went, whether it was a restaurant, amusement park, ball game, or even movie, people would start talking to her and telling her their life story. She had a knack for making complete strangers feel comfortable telling her everything about their lives. She always did her best to be compassionate and offer sound advice.

Hypersensitivity

Some experts have described those with anxiety as being "hyper-sensitive." The hyper-sensitive person usually:

- Has overly sensitive nerves.
- Prefers controlled environments.
- Notices what most people may miss.
- Is extremely empathetic.[20]
- Has overly acute senses.
- Has more sensitive skin.
- Frightens or startle more easily.[21]

By nature, these individuals are ultra-sensitive to their own environment; they notice when anything is out of place. Their head is on a swivel, and they can detect the slightest hint of danger. But most importantly, they care deeply about others and often demonstrate love and compassion to their loved ones and members of their community.

Empathy

Recognizing the stress and anxiousness in your own life could be a catalyst for being compassionate and empathetic toward others. Those who are anxious may have a predisposition to think of others first and have a desire to help and lift their family, friends, and neighbors. Research indicates that those who are anxious are often more empathetic because of their own difficulties and struggles. These personal challenges could inspire a person to be more kind, sensitive, and compassionate to those around them.[22]

Compassion

Those who are compassionate are sympathetic and concerned for the sufferings and the misfortunes of others.[23] Anxious people often possess this trait, perhaps because they have quietly suffered and struggled for years and they are sensitive to those who also seem to struggle. Some have argued that being kind and compassionate to others can provide the anxious person with a sense of purpose and can alleviate their suffering. In fact, most will find that when they put the needs of others before their own, their own anxiety seems to dissipate.

A man whom we will call Brandon shared the following experience:

> I was a graduate student years ago, and I also taught high school full time. To accommodate those who were in the teaching profession, this university graduate program offered classes on Friday evenings and Saturday mornings. In fact, classes ran on Friday from about 4:00 p.m. until about 9:00 p.m., and on Saturday from 8:00 a.m. to about 1:00 p.m. Therefore, the advantage was that I was only in classes two weekends a month instead of every week. Furthermore, Friday/Saturday classes did not interfere with as many activities—at least at that point in my life. One weekend of classes, however, in this program, was the equivalent of two to three weeks of coursework at a normal university—so, missing a Friday or Saturday was out of the question.
>
> On a particular Saturday morning in the fall, following our Friday night classes the evening before, I got a late start for my classes—it was usually about an hour drive from our home to the university. When I jumped into the car, the first thing I noticed was that the gas gauge was close to empty. But since I was running late, I knew that if I stopped to get gas, I would be late to class. Besides, I felt that I probably had enough gas to get to class, and then on the way home I could fill the tank of the car.
>
> As I remember, it was a stressful ride to the campus because I couldn't take my eyes off the gas gauge. Eventually,

I was about five miles from the campus, and I noticed the gas gauge was showing empty. However, I assumed I could go for quite a way in my Subaru wagon with little gas in the tank. Boy was I wrong. About three miles from the campus, I ran out of gas. I was livid! I knew that this would be a big problem. I understood that by the time I walked to the gas station, borrowed a gas can, and then walked back to my car, put the gas in the tank, and then drove back to the station to fill up, I would probably miss the first hour of my class—if not the first two hours.

Of course, as a certified worrier, I believed that being one hour late to class meant I would probably fail the midterm and, consequently, fail the class. I would then have to take the class again, and then probably run out of gas again, and of course, fail the class again. I also believed because I ran out of gas, I would need to live like a hobo under a bridge for the rest of my life. That's how worriers think. Anyway, I began walking to the gas station, which was about one mile away. Once I arrived at the station, I borrowed a gas tank, filled it up, and then walked the mile back to my car. I put the gas in, got the car started, and then drove to the gas station to return the tank and fill up my car.

I was quite mad at myself at this point. I knew that I could have avoided this entire fiasco if I had just filled up the car with gas near my home earlier in the morning. I took a gamble and completely blew it. As I began to fill my car with gas, I pondered how terrible my life was and how being an hour late to a graduate class was about the worst thing that could happen to a human.

As I was thinking was about my tragic life, I noticed that someone was calling for me. I heard a voice saying something like, "Hey, could you help me?" I turned from the gas pump where I was standing, and across the lane at the next row of pumps was the ugliest station wagon I've ever seen. At that point, I saw the man in the driver's seat, who looked like a cross between a pirate and someone who just escaped from prison. I went over to his car and leaned against the driver's side door to hear him more distinctly. He said, "Hey, could you help me fill up my car with gas?" At first, I was a little leery of this man. I wondered if he was really a serial killer who wanted to throw me in his car and drive away. However, I felt he was harmless, so I said, "Sure, what do you need?" He then said, "Could you get my wheelchair down from the top of the car for me? Once you get it down, I can do the rest."

It didn't take long to notice from the looks of his car that he probably lived in it. I felt embarrassed that I hadn't noticed the huge wheelchair strapped to the top of his station wagon. I untied it, and then brought it down to the ground. I held the wheelchair steady until he climbed in. As I was helping him towards the back of his vehicle, I noticed a bumper sticker on his car that read, "Vietnam Vet." It was then that I realized that this man was paralyzed because of an injury he received in the war—defending the very country that allowed me to live a peaceful life.

After getting him situated and then helping him get the wheelchair back on top of his car, I got back in my own car and began the fifteen-minute drive to the campus. At this point, I was well over an hour late for class. However, I don't remember if I ever felt happier going to a college class. First, my happiness came from the simple act of serving someone in need. Second, my happiness was fed by my tremendous sense of gratitude. Here I was, a healthy, fully functioning husband and father. I had a beautiful wife who I adored and three small children at the time—all healthy and happy. I had a home in one of the nicest parts of town. I had a car that didn't look like a reject from a demolition derby. I had a job that I loved. I was in graduate school.

After spending a few minutes with that Vietnam vet, I knew my life was full and rich and wonderful. I didn't have anything to complain about—life was good. Walking into class late that day was not a problem at all. I realized I had learned more at the gas station that day than I would that entire semester in graduate school.

I also learned that when we find someone distressed, in trouble, and in a worse situation than we are, to go and help that person. All too soon, as we are engaged in the act of helping, we will find that our own problems have dissipated. We will feel happiness, joy, and peace.

So, for those of you who are anxious, take heart! One of your great gifts could be making others' lives better and happier, which, in turn, will help you feel joy and happiness.

Conclusion

Being empathetic, caring, and demonstrating concern for others are wonderful traits. Since those who are anxious are often in tune to the needs of others, they may have feelings or impressions that they should reach out and help someone. If you have these feelings, follow them—they usually lead to something wonderful. Being able to grieve with those who grieve, and sorrow with those who are sorrowful is one of the greatest gifts in this life. To walk in someone else's shoes is to be truly empathetic. We recommend that you continue to develop this most amazing gift!

Questions for Thought

1. Does your anxiety motivate you to care for and exercise charity toward others?
2. Have you ever done something kind for someone and recognized that anxiety was a catalyst for your kindness?
3. Has your anxiety ever facilitated feelings of empathy for another person?

SUPERPOWER 3

The Spidey Sense

Instead of worrying about what you cannot control, shift your energy to what you can create.

—ROY BENNETT [24]

Did you know that people with anxiety are just like Spider-Man? Sadly, we are not similar in the web-slinging sense, although that would be great. However, we do share one key ability; we have the spidey sense. For those of you who are unfamiliar with this power, the spidey sense is a tingling feeling in the back of Spider-Man's skull that presents a psychological awareness of Spider-Man's surroundings. It allows Spider-Man to detect danger before it happens. Some call this intuition, or a sixth sense, as we have discussed before. We believe that those who are anxious have this sense to some extent. It is not uncommon for individuals with anxiety to be aware of or sense things before they happen—especially dangerous things. Those with anxiety are sensitive to the sights, smells, and the general aura of their surroundings. In some ways, their head is on a swivel, anticipating what could possibly go wrong.

For example, have you ever selected the seat at a restaurant that has the best view of the entire establishment? Have you ever seemed more aware about potential dangers in locations with large crowds than those you are with? Have you ever had the sense to move away from something, just before the lightning struck the tree and it fell right where you were standing? If this sounds like you, then congratulations; you have anxiety spidey sense.

What Do the Experts Say?

Often, those with anxiety are hypervigilant and aware of their surroundings. They also seem to have a radar detector for impending danger. Sometimes we make fun of these "George Banks" type characters who always wear their seat belts, drive within the speed limit, and put on their turn signal a mile before an intersection. Yes, these individuals are often cautious, perhaps overly cautions, but they are trying to protect themselves and others from danger.

This claim that people with anxiety have a form of spidey sense is corroborated by modern scientific studies. Lindsay George and Lusia Stopa found that individuals with high social anxiety were more aware of their surroundings and potential dangers than individuals with lower levels of social anxiety.[25] This study was supported by another study done by Gilboa-Schechtman and colleagues, who found that highly anxious individuals show a greater enhancement of detecting angry versus happy targets in a crowd.[26]

These specific studies are indicative of a common finding among research regarding anxiety: that anxiety can function as an early warning alarm system. Victoria Lemie Beckner, a clinical psychologist and associate clinical professor at the University of California, San Francisco, stated, "Anxiety is not random. It's not some faulty switch or illness or weakness. Anxiety is part of your healthy, adaptive alarm system."[27] David Barlow, psychologist and professor emeritus at Boston College, has used similar language to describe anxiety, saying it "is the body's alarm system."[28] FamilyDoctor.org, an AAFP award-winning consumer website that provides basic medical information from the American Academy of Family Physicians, has also used the "alarm system" metaphor in their definition of anxiety. Part of the website's entry on generalized anxiety disorder states that "normal feelings of anxiety often serve as an 'alarm system' that alerts you to danger. Your heart may beat fast. Your palms may get sweaty. Anxiety can provide an extra spark to help you get out of danger."[29] Indeed, anxiety can often serve as a radar detector, warning of impending danger and potential threats.

What Does the Spidey Sense Feel Like?

With all this talk of spidey sense and alarm systems, we assume many of you are wondering what this feels like when it is triggered. Beckner explained what this process usually feels like when she said,

> If your brain perceives a threat or danger to you (fire!), it will trigger defensive survival circuitry in the brain (this is a non-conscious process of threat detection and response that occurs in the amygdala). The sirens ring out—that subjective "feeling" of anxiety or fear we all know so well! Meanwhile, the body's internal firefighters are deployed: The sympathetic nervous system activates various organs (increasing heart rate, breathing) and stress hormones are released to increase oxygen and blood sugar levels to prepare the body for action. All these changes in the brain and body create an urgent, powerful drive to act—to do whatever you can to escape the looming menace.

While this is a wonderful way of describing anxiety acting as an alarm system, we must note that not all anxiety reactions work in this fashion. Brayden explained,

> When my anxiety alarm system starts firing, my thoughts begin to either race or slow down, and my head begins to feel hotter. The rest of my body is not necessarily impacted, my breathing does not really change, I do not sweat more, and I don't get more fidgety. This is how my personal system reacts. Others might have a similar experience, while others may have a completely different experience.

The point is to understand what the range of signs are that indicate your anxiety alarm system (spidey sense) is firing and learn how to harness that biological reaction.

Brayden's Experience with Anxiety Spidey Sense

Brayden shared the following personal experience:

My family loves going to Six Flags Over Texas whenever we have our whole family home. My family members are all big fans of roller coasters, except for me; therefore, I always get outvoted when we decide what to do. This is something we have done as a family for many years, but the most recent trip was a little different for me. We went to Six Flags over the Christmas holiday because our whole family was in town. I had been really contemplating my anxiety and truly seeing how I functioned with it from day to day. With introspective analysis running in the back of my mind, I noticed something when we entered Six Flags and began to walk around. The best way I can describe it was feeling like I was in Iron Man's helmet, having Jarvis analyze and categorize each person and face that I saw as we walked around the amusement park. I know, I know, a different superhero reference, but since both Spider-Man and Iron Man are in the Marvel universe, I'm going to use it.

As we walked around Six Flags, my family was seemingly oblivious to the people around us, chatting about which rides to go on next and comparing different wait times. I half-heartedly participated in these conversations. My attention was on the people who stood and walked around us as I subconsciously analyzed everyone and weighed the possibility of potential threats in this crowded location. I realized this was something I had always done when I was in a crowded location and assumed everyone engaged in this practice. When I shared this with my family, I quickly found out that this was not the case.

Ironically, the other individuals in my family who have some anxiety immediately agreed and said they also had their radars going to some extent. On the other hand, those in my family who do not have anxiety were perplexed and surprised that I felt the need to constantly analyze the environment we were in. This is where I came up with the name of this superpower. When I was explaining it to my dad, who doesn't have a drop of anxiety in him, he said, "Oh okay, so it's like your anxiety has a spidey sense?" This statement made me laugh at first but then got me thinking and, voila, the result of that conversation is this chapter.

Brayden then shared this second experience:

> The second story is a prime example of how someone with anxiety and someone without anxiety might react to a potentially hostile situation. My dad and I were in a packed theater about to watch a movie. As we sat down, I noticed an individual who seemed a bit off to me. He was clearly drunk and pretty unkempt, and my spidey sense instantly went off. Throughout the movie, I heard him making noises and shifting around. Some people around him got up and left. I could tell people had made complaints to the management because a theater employee came in a couple times and stood at the front of the theater, watching this man.
>
> Nothing suspicious happened, thank goodness, and as the end credits rolled, my dad and I got up and left. My dad made comments on the movie and asked what I thought. I reflected back and honestly could not remember much about the movie. My focus had been lasered in on the individual who had triggered my spidey sense for much of the movie. My dad was confused and hadn't even noticed the man. In hindsight, this was one of the first times I genuinely thought that there might be something different about how I perceived events compared to other people.

This superpower of anxiety can be seen as a blessing and a curse. However, you can take action to maximize the potential benefits and avoid the downsides. One of the best things you can do is learn what triggers your spidey sense. We'll call this the internal alarm system for this section, and we'll discuss which scenarios may cause your internal alarm system to be on high alert. As Francis Bacon once said, "Knowledge is power,"[30] and understanding how and when your internal alarm system might go off will go a long way in helping you make sense of this aspect of anxiety.

Another way to maximize your internal alarm system is to lean into it. Brayden observed:

> For most of my life, I saw this as a weird part of me that made things harder instead of easier. However, as I began to understand my internal alarm system better and opened my eyes to the benefits it brings, I began to appreciate what it did for me. I have found that as I lean into this part of my anxiety more, I am more aware of those I'm around and can react quicker to potential threats. I have also seen how it helps me notice social cues more easily, therefore allowing me to react to situations with the correct emotion and avoid misunderstandings.

Beckner summarized this concept effectively when she said, "Suppose a car wanders into your lane of traffic, or you develop a cough in these times of COVID-19, or your manager looks away when you say hello. It's a very good thing that your brain is wired to instantly recognize these cues as potentially threatening so that your alarm system is activated to respond protectively. You swerve out of the car's path, call your doctor, or set up a meeting with your manager to check in pronto."[31]

The last way you can maximize your internal alarm system is realizing that most things that trigger your alarm system do not end up causing any harm. This can be seen in a study done by researchers at Penn State who found that only about 8 percent of the things people worry about come true.[32] Knowing that over 91 percent of the things you worry about will not happen should help you from becoming overwhelmed with potentially hostile outcomes that your internal alarm system presents to you. Instead of seeing your internal alarm as constantly presenting issues, you can see it more as Jarvis in Iron Man's helmet—presenting you with information that helps you understand your current setting and the people around you.

Conclusion

If you have anxiety, you share a superpower with Spider-Man. People with anxiety have the spidey sense that allows them to be far more aware of their surroundings, which allows them to react quicker to potentially hostile dangerous or even mildly uncomfortable situations. To be around someone with anxiety is to be around a person who is, essentially, an early warning system for potential danger. This is such a valuable asset to have. Embrace your anxiety, and maximize your own personal spidey sense.

Questions for Thought

1. How would you describe your situational awareness in different settings?
2. Have you ever reacted quicker than everyone else when something happens, be it a hostile situation or something as simple as somebody dropping a plate of food or spilling a drink?
3. Do you ever think of potential outcomes of an upcoming event or excursions in public places?

SUPERPOWER 4

The Analytical Mind

Nothing in life is to be feared. It is only to be understood. Now is the time to understand more, so that we may fear less.

—MARIE CURIE[33]

Did you relate to Brayden feeling like he was Iron-Man wearing his helmet, with Jarvis talking to him and analyzing the world around him? If so, this chapter on the analytical mind is for you. People with anxiety are good at examining things in detail to discover more about themselves so they can place these things within their world. This is usually catalyzed by a worry stimulus that is a prominent symptom of anxiety.

When Brayden was walking around the amusement park feeling like Iron-Man, the worry aspect of his anxiety caused his brain to go into Jarvis-analysis mode so that he could obtain the most detail about his surroundings in order to understand the environment around him. This analytical examination is applied to most aspects of an anxious person's life. However, it is commonly categorized by a negative outlook because it is fueled by worry. This chapter will demonstrate that the analytical mind is not only useful in negative situations. You can change your mindset around the application of the analytical mind so that it truly becomes a superpower.

What Is an Analytical Mind?

The phrase "analytical mind" was thrown around quite a bit in the introduction of this book. What does "analytical mind" mean?

The Merriam-Webster dictionary defines analytical as "of or relating to analysis or analytics . . . separating something into component parts or constituent elements."[34] That feels like a defining salt as salty. Going a step further into the definitions, Merriam-Webster defines analysis as "a detailed examination of anything complex in order to understand its nature or to determine its essential features: a thorough study."[35] Now that we have broken "analytical" down, let's see how it meshes with the mind to form the "analytical mind." Everyone's favorite website, *Indeed*, offers a good explanation for the "analytical mind":

> A method for analyzing a problem and finding a solution. This is a way for processing and breaking down complex information. Analytical thinking is helpful in identifying cause and effect relationships and making connections between two factors. For instance, someone may use analytical thinking to understand the relationship between sunflowers and humidity. To do this, they may ask, *"Why do sunflowers have trouble growing when there's humidity in the air?"*[36]

After a review of the definition of "analytical" and seeing how this concept meshes with the mind in analytical thinking, we can soundly define the analytical mind. Essentially, an analytical mind is a mind that likes to gather as much information as possible so that patterns and relationships between different variables can be found or solutions to problems can be ascertained. The analytical mind is all about information—information that will help an individual make sense of their world, their problems, their identity, and so forth. With this understanding in place, we can now analyze how anxiety and an analytical mind mix.

Anxiety and an Analytical Mind

To understand the relationship between anxiety and an analytical mind, we must understand one of the main symptoms of anxious individuals: worry. *Harvard Health* defines worry as a "component of anxiety symptoms."[37] This relationship between worry and anxiety is also corroborated by definitions regarding anxiety given by Johns Hopkins[38] and the Mayo Clinic.[39]

So, how does worry, a prominent aspect of anxiety, correlate with the analytical mind? Clinical psychologist and founder of *Anxiety Solutions* Dr. Michael Stein said it best when he explained that anxiety can promote the formation of a worry cycle that results in the brain switching to analysis mode in order to resolve the uncertainty created by the worry cycle.[40] It should be noted that this cycle, from worry to analysis, can be potentially harmful when dealing with anxiety symptoms because this cycle can perpetuate our anxiety instead of resolving it. However, for the purpose of this chapter, we will zero in on how worry catalyzes analytical thinking. This relationship has been an essential part of human evolution. In an article published in *Scientific American*, Victoria Stern states, "Psychologists believe that worry, defined as a person's negative thoughts about a future event, evolved as a constructive problem-solving behavior."[41] Hence, worry can spur us into action; in fact, worry can help us find resolution to our problems.

There is, however, a downside to this co-evolution of worry and analysis. As stated previously, the worry that prompts an analytical mindset is often associated with events that can negatively impact an individual. This is evident in a study by Nur Hani Zainal and Michelle G. Newman that found that individuals with generalized anxiety disorder (GAD) displayed more accurate overall reasoning and cognitive reasoning than a control group without GAD, although this was only in relation to negative stimuli or signals.[42] So, how can analytical thinking be a superpower? Pressed further, if the worry symptom of anxiety that catalyzes the analytical mind is primarily correlated with negative outcomes that could potentially promote greater anxiety, how could this be beneficial? When harnessed correctly, the analytical mind can become the greatest problem-solving apparatus for every situation in your life and promote a greater understanding of the world around you.

The Analytical Mind—A Superpower

Despite all the negative aspects associated with worry and anxiety, there are reasons to be positive about what this anxiety can do for you. Towson University psychologist and professor Bethany Pace put a positive spin on worry:

> While many of us are intuitively aware that worry makes us anxious and upset, research shows that we still tend to lean on worry when facing problems in our lives. One reason for this is that we may worry as a way to feel emotionally prepared for negative outcomes. However, another reason—which feels particularly relevant now—is that people often conflate worry with problem solving.[43]

The problem-solving capabilities prompted by anxiety can be a powerful tool in our lives, but we must use that worry to generate action, not let it paralyze us. This can be seen in the following experience shared by Brayden:

> A couple years ago, I found myself in a very tough situation. I had just decided to quit my job in California and move back to Utah so I could focus on some mental health issues that I thought I had resolved. I had no job lined up and no place to live. My anxiety was spiking, and I was very worried about solving these issues. I could have let the worry paralyze me; however, I used it to instigate action. I gathered as much information as I could on how I could resolve the issues that were causing me anxiety. I was blessed to have family in Utah who invited me to live with them while I figured out these issues. With a place to stay and loving family support, I could focus on my other issues. I reached out to all the contacts in my network, looked towards previous jobs, and spent much of my time on job sites. I used my network of friends and family in Utah to try and find a permanent place to live. Essentially, I gathered all the information I could regarding the issues I was

presented with so that I could make a detailed analysis of my options. After acquiring all the information, I analyzed the information I had, found the best path forward, and acted on it. Looking back, the path I chose was the best possible solution, and I am still reaping the benefits of that decision years later.

In this experience, Brayden used the worry brought on by his anxiety to catalyze the formation of an analytical problem-solving approach that allowed him to make the best decision in a hard time. This is how the analytical mind can be seen as a superpower. In fact, this is how you can benefit from your anxiety. You have a built-in problem-solving mechanism that, if used correctly, can help find the best solution to any problem you are faced with. Now that is something special!

Another way the analytical mind can be seen as a superpower is by collecting the information you are able to attain through the implementation of this thought process. Brayden illustrates this with another significant experience:

When I was in college, I spent a summer as a youth counselor for my church. This was a couple years after I had had my first real traumatic experience with anxiety, and I was beginning to have a change of heart regarding my anxiety and how it impacted me. This was made very prevalent in my interactions with the youth over the course of that summer. When I would meet the young men that I had responsibility for, I would have some anxiety because I was worried about being the best counselor I could be for those kids. This triggered my analytical mind, and subconsciously my brain would use analytical problem-solving to resolve the worry. And, as was stated earlier in this chapter, what does analysis thrive on? The collection of information. This resulted in me doing my best to get to know these young men and truly trying to understand them and where they come from. Because of this information gathering, I was able to address the needs of these kids in a personalized manner and help them in ways I never could have if I hadn't had taken the time to get to know them, empathize with them, and learn from them. Because of this, many of the young men would come talk to me one-on-one at the conclusion of the weeklong camp and thank me for truly trying to get to know them and being able to address individual worries and problems that they were dealing with. These interactions were very touching to me and were some of the most fulfilling experiences I have ever had.

Brayden successfully used the information he gathered using the analytical mind to connect with and build genuine relationships with the youth he was in charge of. Many people with anxiety do not recognize they have this skill. The more we know, the more power and capacity we have. Furthermore, there are few things that help a person to attain more knowledge and information than the analytical mind of an individual with anxiety. In this way, the analytical mind is once again seen to be a superpower.

How Do I Hone My Analytical Mind?

You may be thinking, "How can I negate the negative aspects of the analytical mind and maximize the benefit?" In this section we will lay out four ways you can do exactly that.

1. Don't let worry paralyze you; instead, use that worry as fuel to act. Many people get stuck in the worry cycle because they overanalyze a situation. Their anxiety overwhelms them, and, consequently, they end up doing nothing because they are overwhelmed. Then, they may begin the analysis process all over again in the hopes of finding a simpler answer. Don't let this happen! The Roman poet Horace said, "Don't think, just do." That needs to be a part of your mentality.[44] When you have used the problem-solving analysis to gather information regarding a situation that is causing you to feel anxious and worry, formulate a solution based on the information you have gathered, and then act. Go! Do! Trust your instincts. Although it might be hard at first, the more you act on the solutions you have identified, the more you will see how your analysis alleviates worry and anxiety, and you will begin to trust the process more.

2. Don't dwell on the negative; find the good. The worry we feel is stimulated by perceived negative stimuli. This often leads us to dwell on the negatives and results in an overall negative frame through which we enact the analytical mind. However, this does not have to be the case. Journalist Josh L. Doman said it well:

> If there are devils, there are surely angels. Washing away the evil and negative thoughts with good and positive ones will train your mind to blacken out these rascals as soon as they enter your mind. Going to "happy" environments and entering your "good" state of mind (e.g. listening to music, doing a certain activity, being gratified) will also be helpful in shifting the focus.[45]

Replace the negative thoughts with positive ones. If you are presented with a negative situation, use your analytical mind to find resolutions that could change the negative situation into a positive one. Certainly, how you perceive things matters and you need to train your brain to focus on the good instead of the bad. We realize this is difficult for people with anxiety. In fact, it took both of us several years to retrain our brains. But trust us, it is worth it. If you can frame the application of your analytical mind within a lens of positivity, then there are few circumstances that can't be changed to a positive.

3. Retrain your brain to be more positive through repetition. Consider this question: How did I become so pessimistic, or so worried, about every little thing? We all become anxious through repetition—thinking of negative thoughts, worst case scenarios, or horrible outcomes repeatedly. Mark shared the following experience:

> One day I was driving with my children in the car. Some of them were now teenagers, so they were extremely interested in paying close attention to every detail while I was driving. I owned a stick-shift (manual transmission) car at the time, and my children had many questions about the gear shift and the clutch.

As I was driving around a sharp curve in the road, one of my children said, "Dad, how did you do that?" I responded, "How did I do what?" One of my daughters said, "As we went around that curve, you shifted the gears (I was downshifting), pressed in and let out the clutch, put on the blinker, and turned the volume down on the car stereo—all at the same time." I actually thought, "Wait, I did all of that? Pretty cool, actually." I explained to my daughter that I was able to do all of that because of repetition. I had done all of those movements and manipulations thousands of times, so it was second nature to me.

On a higher level, I had created a neural pathway—a macro of sorts—so that when my eyes saw a curve in the road, my brain knew exactly what to do and performed all of those functions automatically, without me paying close attention to what was happening.

Each of us has created thousands of neural pathways so that we can function at a high level. These pathways help us act and think in certain ways when we encounter specific situations. For example, if any of us were jogging down a mountain trail and saw a bear, we would instinctively run without thinking, "What do I do?" That happens because a neural pathway has been created in our brains, and when danger approaches, we know to get the heck out of there—and fast.

Likewise, we have created thousands of these pathways in our brains that determine how we think about certain things. We encounter stimuli that could cause anxious or fearful thoughts. For example, if it's after midnight and you can't reach your teenagers who still haven't come home, you may think that something terrible has happened. Why? Because you have trained your mind to think of the worst-case scenarios. You may later find out that your child fell asleep at their friend's house watching a movie and they were never in any danger.

So, how do we leverage neural pathways to our advantage? We create new ones—positive pathways that will help us experience the world in a much more pleasant way. How do we create these pathways? One way is repetition. Go to Google or to another source that has inspirational quotations. Make a collection of ten to fifteen statements or quotes that are positive, hopeful, and optimistic. Transfer these statements to a sticky note, a 3x5 card, or your phone or electronic device. Every hour of the day, pause for one minute and review one or two of these statements. Do this every day, each hour, for twenty to thirty days, and you will create a new habit. We believe this is one way that you can change your negative thinking into more positive thoughts and ideas. Over time, we have learned to become negative and pessimistic. Let's reverse that and learn to become more positive and hopeful.

4. Don't think you need to know everything; embrace simplicity. While the information you gather through your application of the analytical mind is necessary, it can sometimes become an insidious factor. Obsessively searching for information can lead you down paths that can divert your attention or derail your confidence in the solutions you have already discovered. Once again, Doman said it perfectly:

> In order to manage your thoughts, you have to keep track on them and break them down. But take note: you can't always include all thoughts. You have to dissect them and choose which ones are noteworthy. Begin with a mind map, or even with sticky notes. This is the time you can use your natural planning ability, characterized by meticulosity and preciseness. This system will help you organize your thoughts. In this way, it can help you discern which ones are worth developing and contributing to your life.[46]

Simplify your thought process and train your brain to only choose thoughts, information, and solutions that are contributing to your life. Block out the noise and focus on the beneficial. This will allow you to stay on track when you are using the analytical mind to find the solution to a problem or to gather information about the world around you.

Conclusion

In this chapter, we have attempted to show how the analytical mind of people with anxiety can become a superpower. Through the studies we have addressed, definitions we have provided, experiences we have shared, and advice we have given, we hope that you can see how the analytical mind can help your own anxiety become a superpower.

Questions for Thought

1. Has there been a time in your life where you have used the analytical mind to find a solution to a problem?
2. Does worry cause you to act or does it incapacitate you? What can you do to change that?
3. How can you implement the analytical mind with your own anxiety moving forward?

SUPERPOWER 5

The Nurturing Leader

Do not anticipate trouble or worry about what may never happen. Keep in the sunlight.

—BENJAMIN FRANKLIN[47]

Surprisingly, those who are anxious are often not just good leaders, but great ones. People like Abraham Lincoln and Winston Churchill suffered from anxiety. However, they did not let their anxiousness shut them down as leaders. They simply plowed ahead and forged a path that led them to success.

Individuals who have anxiety are often people-centered, kind, warm, empathetic, intuitive, goal driven, and caring. Believe it or not, anxious people can be great leaders, especially if they can contain some anxious qualities that are not so appealing, like panicking over minor situations, controlling others, worrying excessively, seeking perfectionism, micromanaging, and always seeing the negative in every situation.

Morra Aarons-Mele, author of *The Anxious Achiever: Turn Your Biggest Fears Into Your Leadership Superpower,* explained, "When you understand your anxiety and learn to leverage it, you develop a leadership superpower. When you are attuned to your emotions and what they are trying to tell you, you become self-aware, conscious and a thoughtful leader."[48]

Many great leaders have made anxiety their superpower. High achievers and strong leaders are prone to stress and anxiety, and that's okay! Anxiety can also be viewed as a strength, not merely a weakness. Consider some of the following leadership strengths.

Watchmen on the Tower

Anxiety looks forward to the future. Those who are anxious often worry about what can happen down the road—they are incredible predictors and forecasters. Scott Stossel, editor of the *Atlantic*, made this point: "Anxious people, because they are vigilantly scanning the environment for threats, tend to be more attuned than adrenaline junkies to other people's emotions and signals."[49] Morra Aarons-Mele added, "[Anxious leaders] are always thinking about and anticipating what's next. This is an incredible skill for leaders because we always need to come up with creative ways to meet future challenges."[50] Because anxiety is often manifest in anticipation, anxious leaders are always looking on the horizon, predicting problems before they arise, and prescribing proactive solutions.

The Analytical Mind

Those who have anxiety are often blessed with an analytical mind—a mind that seems to never shut off. The anxious leader will often wake up at 4:00 a.m. with ideas for their business coursing through their minds. In her book *Good Anxiety: Harnessing the Power of the Most Misunderstood Emotion*, Wendy Suzuki shares the experience of Dev and Monica. Dev was an entrepreneur, and Monica was a business development consultant. In a business conversation, Monica admitted to Dev that she has suffered from anxiety for most of her professional career. She would "obsess over every move and every last decision in her early years. It nearly made her search for a new way of making a living."[51]

Monica then shared with Dev her secret to her success.

> She said that she realized that all her obsessive tendencies that led her to worry and question every move were actually a major advantage in her business and her life. . . . She realized that when she was under pressure . . . to make a deal, she could train her attention to identify all the possible pitfalls in a particular situation. She realized that rather than blow off that instinct, she could actually use it to create a

list of possible scenarios to analyze. This strategy worked for her business decisions and life decisions. She realized that her what-if list wasn't actually a sign that she was losing her touch; it was a tool to help her do a more effective and complete evaluation of any business proposition at hand. . . . She had taught herself how to use the agitation of her good anxiety to drill down . . . on her business decisions and dealings. As she remarked to Dev, "Embracing my anxiety has made me a much more effective entrepreneur."[52]

Having an analytical mind that races hundreds of miles per hour is not always a bad thing. That analytical mind can help a leader fixate on problems, consider possible solutions, and then go to work.

Ready, Set, Go!

Another great leadership trait of the anxious individual is taking action. Think about it. If you really feared something, would you simply sit there in fear, or would you do something about it? If you knew that a hurricane was heading toward your community, wouldn't you do something? Wouldn't you either flee (if there was time) or board up your home and protect it from the elements? Anxiety can certainly inspire leaders to act in order to solve a problem.[53] Morra Aarons-Mele wrote, "Anxious achievers are goal-oriented, future-oriented and prized team members because we go the extra mile, and nothing less than the best will do."[54]

One author observed, "So anxiety isn't useless. In an economic crisis, the anxiety that keeps us up at night may help us fathom a solution to keeping our business open."[55] The anxious leader will not sit still in a crisis. They will go and do, and in the process, move the organization forward.

Honesty and Openness

Anxious people, and anxious leaders, are often open and honest. These leaders would be the first to say, "I don't know how we are going to fix this" or "I am not certain what the future could look like." Their candor and honesty are often refreshing and certainly endearing. People are drawn to leaders who are honest with their feelings.[56] The anxious are often humble and meek, aware of their own shortcomings. Furthermore, the anxious leader would have no trouble asking coworkers and subordinates for help, perspective, and new ideas.

Having a Plan and Working Hard

Anxious people, and anxious leaders, have a plan. The anxious leader will say, "Okay, team, here is what we are going to do." Because anxious individuals do not like surprises and want to be prepared, they are often planners. Anxious leaders also like structure, plans, and strategizing. The anxious do not like inaction; instead, they will find a plan or a solution, and forge ahead.

Furthermore, because the anxious do not like to be ill prepared, they work hard and effectively because they want to be ready. Morra Aarons-Mele explained, "Anxiety loves a goal. When you can direct your anxiety toward a specific task, you'll pour all that yearning and energy into attention to detail, thoroughness, and lots of practice. You won't miss deadlines and you'll rock the final product."[57]

Anxious leaders do not want to look stupid or ill prepared. To avoid that kind of stress, they can be overprepared and ready for any task at hand.

Thinking Outside the Box

Anxious people can be creative. The possibilities for solutions to problems are endless. Alison Beard, an author in the *Harvard Business Review*, wrote:

> Talking about a particularly difficult period during 1862, Lincoln explained that "we had about played our last card and must change tactics or lose the game!" Certainly, he tried all kinds of possibilities to save the Union during the first two years of the Civil War—from appointing different Union generals to issuing the Emancipation Proclamation. Roosevelt experimented with an alphabet soup of policies

to shore up the larger economy and improve American lives in the Great Depression. During the Cuban Missile Crisis in 1962, President John F. Kennedy had a similar strategy: He assembled a group of experts and offered them the latitude to try to solve the problem without an escalation into nuclear war. Of course, in times of great challenge, you often find that more of your moves don't work than do.[58]

The anxious are able "to think broadly across multiple ideas all at once."[59] They tend to think divergently—there are a hundred different ways to skin a cat—and the anxious leader has the potential to find multiple solutions.

Attuned and Empathetic Leadership

Anxious leaders are often in tune with the needs of those around them, and they can feel and express empathy to those whom they lead. To be in tune—to know when others are sad, afraid, unhappy, fearful, hurt, or experiencing grief—is one of the great traits of any leader. Empathy—to be able to relate to others, and to have "walked in their shoes"—is one of the greatest gifts of human relations and leadership. Morra Aarons-Mele wrote, "Anxious people can be very empathetic and are good at tuning into personal or group dynamics. When we're anxious, we're concerned about what other people think about us, and we're constantly searching for clues. . . . We can also manage people better. Because I knew how I reacted when I was anxious at work, I was better able to help other people manage their leadership anxiety."[60]

Conclusion

Can anxious people be great leaders? They certainly can! We have highlighted many of the reasons anxiety makes great leaders. They are analytical, they are in tune with the needs of others, they work hard to squish problems before they bubble to the surface, and they have the gift of intuition. So, if you are a leader in any capacity—professionally, at home, in a congregation, or in the community—know that your skills and abilities are not only appreciated and respected, but sought after. You are the type of leader that people will want to follow.

Questions for Thought

1. Are you aware of any leaders in your life who struggle with anxiety?
2. In your opinion, how can anxiety create great leaders?
3. How can some of your most anxious traits help you become a great leader?

SUPERPOWER 6

Self-Awareness

Knowing yourself is the beginning of wisdom.
—ARISTOTLE[61]

Some people have a low social IQ, while others seem to be very aware of themselves and others. For example, imagine a man named Steve has just come home from the hospital. His wife, who was in her mid-thirties, just died from colon cancer, leaving Steve and three young children in a state of shock. Shortly after Steve enters his home, a neighbor comes over, complaining that Steve's three young children were playing in her yard. As the neighbor complains, Steve listens in disbelief. His wife passed away just an hour or two ago. Steve, who does have the gift of awareness, listens nicely to the neighbor and then says, "Don't worry, I'll take care of it," to shut down the conversation.

Many of us, however, would love to say something like, "Hey, you jerky neighbor, don't you know my wife died an hour ago? And really? You're mad that my children walked through your yard? Your dog has done his business in my yard many times, and we have never complained!"

Self-awareness really does play a significant role in our day-to-day interactions with ourselves and those around us. We certainly need to be connected to our own thoughts, feelings, passions, and beliefs.

Do you understand yourself? How aware are you of the thoughts, feelings, and characteristics that define you? People have been asking these questions for centuries. The phrase "know thyself" was famously inscribed at the temple of Apollo in ancient Delphi thousands of years ago and is considered one of the most important Delphic maxims ever written. The question "who am I?" resounds across time and generations and has led to several explanations from some of the greatest philosophers, theologians, and writers the world has seen. Being self-aware, being able to understand yourself to your core, is a powerful concept. Moreover, becoming self-aware is also something that people with anxiety are very good at figuring out.

Self-awareness has become an interesting topic of discussion in our modern day. Merriam-Webster[62] defines self-awareness as "an awareness of one's own personality and individuality." You would think in our era where individuality is celebrated and living a life that is compatible with our values is lauded that this definition would mean that we celebrate being self-aware as a critical aspect of our development. However, many in our contemporary world, especially those with anxiety, see self-awareness as a negative. We associate self-awareness with increased anxiety and an inability to feel satisfied with who we are as a person. The purpose of this chapter is to push back against this narrative. We will show you that self-awareness can truly be a superpower.

Two Types of Self-Awareness

Before we can fully address self-awareness, we must define the two components that encapsulate being self-aware: *internal self-awareness* and *external self-awareness*. Internal self-awareness is represented by "how clearly we see our own values, passions, aspirations, fit with our environment, reactions (including thoughts, feelings, behaviors, strengths, and weaknesses), and impact on others."[63] External self-awareness "refers to understanding how other people view them based on the same factors listed above—values, aspirations, emotions, behaviors, strengths, weaknesses, environment fit, and the impact they have on others. In addition, externally self-aware individuals have a higher level of empathy and strong social norms."[64] These definitions come from an article written in the *Harvard Business Review* by Dr. Tasha Eurich, who explained why this type of delineation within self-awareness is important. Dr. Eurich wrote:

It's easy to assume that being high on one type of awareness would mean being high on the other. But our research has found virtually no relationship between them. . . . When it comes to internal and external self-awareness, it's tempting to value one over the other. But leaders must actively work on both seeing themselves clearly *and* getting feedback to understand how others see them. The highly self-aware people we interviewed were actively focused on balancing the scale. . . . The bottom line is that self-awareness isn't one truth. It's a delicate balance of two distinct, even competing, viewpoints.[65]

The duality of self-awareness is important to understand if we are to fully embrace this superpower of anxiety. This chapter will refer to both internal and external self-awareness so that we can show you how the development of both aspects brings about the greatest benefit. But first, we need to address an important delineation within self-awareness, the difference between healthy self-awareness and perfectionism.

Perfectionism—The Enemy of Healthy Self-Awareness

Perfectionism is the aspect of self-awareness that correlates with all the negative connotations associated with being self-aware. Dr. Tara Well demonstrated how self-awareness can start positive but drift into negative perfectionism in the following statement from an article in *Psychology Today.*

> Self-awareness seems like a good thing because it allows you to know yourself, understand your motivations, and ultimately make better decisions. But it can also lead you to second guess yourself and spin out into an excruciating state of self-consciousness, micro-analyzing every nuance of your thoughts and actions.[66]

In our opinion, this spiral into an excruciating state of self-consciousness occurs when perfectionism truly kicks in and ramps up our anxiety to unhealthy levels. A recent study corroborated this idea, showing that individuals with higher levels of perfectionism had increased levels of anxiety, especially social anxiety.[67] An article published in the *UPMC Western Behavioral Health Beat* further supported this concept: "Though the exact relationship between anxiety and perfectionism is tricky to untangle, perfectionism and anxiety often go hand in hand. People who've been diagnosed with anxiety, for example, tend to display more perfectionistic traits[68] than the average citizen, according to a meta-analysis published in the *Journal of Clinical Psychology*."[69]

So, what does this connection between anxiety and perfectionism mean? Individuals with anxiety have a higher risk of having healthy self-awareness sabotaged by a descent into unhealthy perfectionism. Brayden shared the following experience on how he found himself falling into this trap.

> One thing that was very important to me while I was growing up was making sure I had good grades. I was very self-aware of how important education was to me, my family, and how much I truly loved to learn. I felt like getting good grades was a good indicator of my own personal success. However, this would sometimes descend into an unhealthy form of perfectionism. For example, after taking a big test, I would obsessively check my grades to see what my score was. There would be times when my mom would even ban me from looking at my grades because I did it too often. If I ever received a grade on a big assignment that I didn't feel was good enough, I would spiral and my anxiety would tell me things like, "You'll never get into a good college now," or, "Good luck graduating high school; you're going to fail out with these kinds of grades." (Side note: I did graduate, and I did end up going to the college of my dreams.) Speaking of college, I remember once during my freshman year, I had just finished taking a test, felt good about it, and ended up getting an 80 out of 100 on it. By all means, this was a decent grade. It was above the average, which was a 75! However, that's not how my perfectionism saw it. I spent the rest of the day moping around campus, considering

how I was either going to flunk out of college or have to end up transferring because I wasn't smart enough to go to this college. Striving to have good grades is a good thing. Being self-aware enough to realize how important good grades are to your own values and personality is also good; however, taking it to the level of perfectionism like I did is not only unhealthy, but it also leads to elevated levels of bad anxiety.

Perfectionism is not true self-awareness; perfectionism is self-awareness taken to an extreme and laced with negative anxiety. This distinction is important to understand because it will help you to pursue true self-awareness and be conscious of when you are beginning to cross over into unhealthy perfectionism. With this delineation in place, we can address true self-awareness and how it is a superpower.

Self-Awareness—Know Thyself

True self-awareness has many benefits. This can be seen in a quote from the *Harvard Research Review*[70] referred to earlier in this chapter. Research suggests that when we see ourselves clearly, we are more confident and more creative.[71] We make sounder decisions,[72] build stronger relationships,[73] and communicate more effectively.[74] We're less likely to lie, cheat, and steal.[75] Sounds like some pretty great benefits if you ask us.

Humber River Health further elaborated on the benefits of self-awareness. Consider the following:

- Being better able to manage and regulate your emotions
- Better communication
- Better decision-making skills
- Improved relationships
- Higher levels of happiness
- More confidence
- Better job satisfaction
- Better leadership skills
- Better overall perspective
- More likely to make better choices[76]

These are all amazing benefits that individuals with strong self-awareness can acquire. And do you want to know the best part? People with anxiety are some of the most self-aware people in the world. Often, we are taught to cope with the negative aspects of anxiety, which allow us to become much more self-aware. Strategies like meditation, journaling, mindfulness, understanding triggers and where they come from, and the self-analysis we so often engage in contribute to greater levels of self-awareness. Brayden shared the following experience about how learning to deal with the negative parts of his anxiety helped him become more self-aware.

> When I first came home from my mission trip and started to really try and learn to deal with my anxiety, a fortunate byproduct was that I learned a lot about myself. Through countless therapy sessions, introspective moments, life analysis, and growing experiences, I was able to come to fully understand who I was as a person. While my anxiety started off as a negative part of my life, it soon became the vehicle by which I was able to become more self-aware. My attempts to understand my anxiety only catalyzed my self-awareness, and I felt that as I learned more about how my particular form of anxiety operated, I learned more about how I as a human functioned. Even though I have reached a point where I have a very strong understanding of my anxiety, I still utilize the tools at my disposal to make sure I stay in touch with who I am. As I look back on the years I have spent with my anxiety, I have realized that in order to keep negative anxiety out of my life and optimize the superpower benefits of anxiety, I need to understand at a fundamental level who I am as a person—my identity!

Understanding anxiety and understanding ourselves are inextricably linked. The more you come to know and understand how your anxiety works, the more self-aware you will become, and the amazing benefits listed above will be yours to have.

You're probably wondering, "How can I make sure I have healthy self-awareness and avoid falling into the trap of perfectionism?" Here are three ways you can make sure you are staying in a healthy self-awareness mindset.

1. Work on how to be kind to yourself. Our internal dialogue plays a huge role in maintaining positive self-awareness and developing internal self-awareness. In a study titled *Not all emotions are created equal: The negativity bias in social-emotional development*, researchers found that there is an asymmetry in our minds where we overwhelmingly linger in negative thinking as opposed to positive thinking.[77] This is something that we need to fight against when we are trying to cultivate positive self-awareness. When you meditate, practice mindfulness, or journal, try to focus on the good and don't overemphasize the bad. It is important to have both in order to create a complete picture of who you are as a person, but it is of lesser importance to dwell overlong on the bad. So, be nice to yourself! Understand that you are human and that being human comes with the good and the bad. Be your own biggest cheerleader and try and maintain an attitude of positivity when you are trying to develop the positive aspects of self-awareness.

2. Make sure you are developing both internal and external self-awareness. The importance of this delineation was addressed above, and we need to work on developing both aspects. Benefits such as improved relationships, more effective communication, and better leadership skills can only be achieved if we have a strong understanding of ourselves *and* how we are perceived by others. Many times, we are much better at one than the other. Brayden has always been very good at internal self-awareness but has had to really work on external self-awareness. Mark is very much the same way. Come to understand which one you are naturally better at and work to develop the opposing aspect so that you can gain the full benefits of this superpower.

3. Seek honest feedback from *loving* critics. This will help you develop external self-awareness and help you to understand areas you need to grow. We emphasized *loving* because loving critics will help you maintain an overall positive self-image while also helping you develop in areas where growth is needed. Brayden related the following experience when it comes to getting honest feedback from loving critics.

> My parents are the honest critics I go to the most. They know me better than anyone else and are always loving in their feedback, even if it is negative. As I have learned that external self-awareness is the aspect I most need help with, I will often talk to my parents and ask them for an honest assessment on how they perceive me and what I can do to change. I will also call them when I feel negative perfectionism entering into my thoughts, and they will help ground me in reality and reaffirm that I am not perceived the way my negative perfectionism has twisted me to think. For example, when I first came home from my mission trip, I assumed that everyone at church thought of me as broken and a failure. My parents were quick to call out this untrue external perception and would ground me in the truth, which was that everyone at church loved me, was worried for me, and wanted to help.

Feedback from loving critics will help ground you, help you to get out of your own head and truly see how you are perceived, and help you grow in areas you may not know you needed growth.

Conclusion

Lao Tzu put it best when he said, "Knowing others is intelligence; knowing yourself is true wisdom."[78] Being self-aware is such a superpower, and people with anxiety are naturally good at this social skill. As long as you neutralize the negative perfectionism in your life and focus on developing positive self-awareness, both internal and external, you will come to see how self-awareness catalyzed by an understanding of your own personal anxiety can be a superpower.

Questions for Thought

1. Have your coping mechanisms for the bad aspects of anxiety helped you become more self-aware?
2. Does it ever bother you when you feel someone else is lacking in self-awareness?
3. Do you know what your personality type is and how it impacts your view of the world?

SUPERPOWER 7

Emergency Preparedness

For someone with anxiety, dramatic situations are, in a way, more comfortable than the mundane. In dramatic situations, the world rises to meet your anxiety.

—MELISSA BRODER[79]

Because the anxious person often anticipates the worst, they are prepared to deal with the unexpected, ready for surprises, and often prepared for emergencies. Mark shared the following experience:

> During the fall semester of my sophomore year of college, my mom called and said my grandfather had passed away. That news was shocking since my grandfather was not even sick. Lucky for him, he died just how he would have wanted. He was bowling with his buddies; he rolled a perfect strike, turned around and celebrated, and then just keeled over. He had a massive heart attack and died doing something he loved.
>
> Because I would be getting married later that spring, it was decided that I would get my grandfather's car. When I went home for Christmas that year, I gave my brother my Pontiac Sunbird, and I took the Dodge Aspen—a grandfather car for sure. When I opened the trunk of the Aspen, I could not believe what I saw. My grandfather was prepared for any emergency! In that trunk, there was a supply of water, an extra tank of gas, flares, tools, blankets, and even some non-perishable food.

I knew my grandfather was a worrier, and the contents of his trunk proved that he was ready for any apocalyptic event, or at a minimum, a flat tire. I had never seen anyone more prepared for an emergency. And his preparation matched his level of anxiety.

If We Are Prepared, We Need Not Fear

Many years ago, religious leader Jeffrey R. Holland wrote,

> As with any other germ, a little preventive medicine ought to be practiced in terms of those things that get us down. There is a line from Dante that says, "The arrow seen before cometh less rudely" (*Divine Comedy*). President John F. Kennedy put the same thought into one of his state of the union messages this way: "The time to repair the roof is when the sun is shining." The Boy Scouts say it best of all: "Be prepared." That isn't just cracker-barrel wisdom with us; it is theology. "And angels shall fly through the midst of heaven, crying with a loud voice. . . . Prepare ye, prepare ye." . . . "But if ye are prepared ye shall not fear" (D&C 38:30). . . . And fear is part of what I wish to oppose this morning. . . . Preparation—prevention if you will—is perhaps the major weapon in your arsenal against discouragement and self-defeat.[80]

Those with anxiety are often the most prepared for any obstacle that can possibly lie in their way. The anxious person often anticipates events and circumstances that could cause them trouble, from taking the wrong road during rush hour traffic, to leaving out tiny toys that could cause an infant to choke. The anxious person certainly lives by the mantra "if something can go wrong, it probably will." We know that sounds fatalistic, and certainly depressing. However, the good news is that many anxious people prepare themselves for such emergencies. They have extra tank of gas in their garage, extra cash in the glove box, a first-aid kit in their backpack, duct tape in their purse, and some superglue in their fanny pack. These people are ready!

Anxiousness Leads to Readiness

French researchers published a study that has shed some more light on anxious people. They found that "anxious individuals detect threat in a different region of the brain from people who are more laid back. It was previously thought that anxiety could lead to oversensitivity to threat signals. However, the new study shows that the difference has a useful purpose. Anxious people process threats using regions of the brain responsible for action."[81] Ellen Hendricksen, author of *How to Be Yourself: Quite Your Inner Critic and Rise Above Social Anxiety*, explained that a certain degree of anxiety "can help people anticipate obstacles, remain cautious and stay organized,"[82] which can all be useful in a crisis.

Isn't it great to know that anxiety can propel us into action? A former high school athlete would often tell his wife, "I am worried about my shoulder; it hurts all the time." His wife would respond, "Instead of worrying about it, why don't you go to the doctor and get it fixed." Now, there is a novel idea—instead of stewing over something that incites fear, or constantly worrying about a problem, why don't we just fix it?

It is our fear that can most often motivate us to be prepared for emergencies. If we are worried that our house may burn down, we can take precautions around our yard to better protect our homes from a fire. If we fear that one of our children may drown in a pool, we can arrange for them to take swimming lessons, or we can build a large fence around our pool. If we are worried about the economy of our country and potential food shortages, we can stockpile food and other supplies in our homes so that we will be ready for a crisis. If we are worried about our financial status, we can meet with a financial advisor, invest our money wisely, and build up an emergency savings account for a rainy day. Peace can come into our lives as we feel prepared for challenges and crises.

Author Alex Ronan wrote about how his anxiety helps him in an emergency:

> When it comes to a sudden emergency, I snap to. For fear of sounding like I'm bragging, I'll just say that I've helped a nice

number of strangers in awful circumstances. My anxiety is always there, humming in the background, sometimes so present I can't listen to anything else. It's a deadweight, one I sometimes wish I could chuck in the Hudson River. But carrying something like that around doesn't only give you a neck ache, it also gives you a particular type of strength.[83]

In Case of Emergency

Indeed, anxiety can be more than a strength; it can be a superpower! Columnist Elizabeth Joyce wrote, "You may think, as someone with anxiety disorders, I'm likely to panic and overreact in the event of any potential threat. But, actually, in a real emergency, I become incredibly business-like and handle the situation quite calmly. This happens when there is a true, external threat because, by its nature of being real and being present, I can take action."[84] Jamie Friedlander explained, "I have generalized anxiety disorder, but in times of true crisis, my anxiety seems to disappear."[85] It is as if, those with anxiety have been prepared for a crisis their entire lives, and when those crisis emerge, these individuals are ready!

Rescue 911

Why are anxious people good in emergencies? There are perhaps several options to consider. First, people who are anxious may feel that they live in a crisis anyway, or under deep levels of stress, so why not have one more crisis? Because these individuals live in a general state of anxiety, stress and crisis have become second nature to them. Mark explained this phenomenon this way:

> I worked at a psychiatric hospital for an internship in graduate school. When families would bring a loved one into the hospital, I began to recognize that this was one of the most significant events in the life of that family. This was a huge day for parents, in some cases, who were bringing their twenty-five-year-old son in to be diagnosed and treated for bi-polar disorder, or perhaps something

even worse. However, for me, it was just another day at the office. In fact, by the time a typical day was over, I would have talked to three people who had attempted suicide, five people who were diagnosed with a major mental illness, and perhaps one person who would be out of control, swearing, physically threatening, and completely distraught. But for me, it was just another day at work.

Because the stress level was so high at this hospital, Mark lived in it, breathed it, and experienced it each day, until what initially could be described as a crisis was now just a "walk in the park."

Second, many individuals with anxiety have learned how to deal with extreme stress and crisis. They have learned interventions such as managing their self-talk, recognizing their mistaken beliefs, deep breathing exercises, relaxation techniques, and how to put their problems in perspective. If these anxious individuals are on their "A" game, they will share their wisdom with others who are overly stressed or anxious. They can use what they have learned to bless and strengthen their family and friends. They have been taught how to navigate a crisis, and now they are ready to use what they have learned.

Third, those who are anxious are often expecting a crisis. Because they can anticipate the worst, they can prepare themselves and others to deal with difficult situations. After all, they have thought about these scenarios many times, and they have mentally rehearsed what they would do if an emergency did occur. Mark shared the following experience that highlights some of these principles:

> In December of 2009, our family traveled from our home in the suburbs of Dallas to the Las Vegas Bowl, where we would watch our son play in his first college bowl game. Incidentally, the Brigham Young University Cougars defeated the Oregon St. Beavers, 44–20. That was on December 22—and that was a great day.
>
> One of our sons who loves being home wanted to leave that night after the bowl game and begin driving. However, I'm quite the cheapskate, and we had paid good money for a hotel on the strip in Vegas. I told my son that I didn't want

to abandon a hotel that we had just paid for. I convinced him that we just needed to get some good rest, and then we could leave around 5:00 a.m. That proved to be a big mistake.

We woke up early on the morning of December 23 and began our drive. We planned to travel all day and through the night, and expected to arrive sometime at our home in McKinney, Texas, in the early morning hours of December 24. That was a great plan. Unfortunately, it didn't happen. As we commenced our drive from Las Vegas to Flagstaff, Arizona, the snow began to fall, and the road conditions became rather tenuous. Although it took longer than it should have, and even though there were many accidents on that stretch of highway, we made it to Flagstaff safely for a brief lunch. However, Flagstaff to Albuquerque, New Mexico, was a different story. The driving conditions became worse with each mile. Instead of traveling at seventy-five miles per hour, we were resigned to creeping along between thirty and forty miles per hour.

Then, from Albuquerque into Amarillo, Texas—usually a four-hour drive—things became intense. Often, I-40 was shut down. There were several stretches where, because of accidents (usually with large eighteen-wheelers), every car was simply parked on the highway. Sometimes cars would be stalled on the side of the road for hours, with no rescue vehicles or tow trucks in sight.

Our goal was to make it home for Christmas, and with each slow mile, we realized that there was a strong possibility we could be stranded in our car on the side of a highway on Christmas Day. There were so many cars that had slid off the road, so many people who needed help, and no help to be found. The number of accidents simply overwhelmed the emergency teams.

We felt helpless, knowing that if we did pull off the highway to render assistance, there was a great chance we would not make it out of the snowbank that was the entire side of the road, and then we could be stranded for a long time.

During one of these stopping points where we had been stranded for hours, I called the Highway Patrol to report one of these accidents. I was basically told that there were so many accidents that there was nothing they could do.

We drove around every parked car and came right up to the accident scene where two large diesel trucks had jackknifed next to each other. There was about a ten-foot gap between the two trucks. I don't know why, but the drivers of all of the cars in front of us saw that narrow gap between the trucks and assumed that it was useless to attempt to drive between them. So, like victims, everyone just sat in the cars, resigned to be there until help arrived.

I think that is when my anxiety kicked in. Rather than sit there with the rest of these "victims," we decided we would take matters into our own hands. We must have been about the tenth car in a long line of vehicles trapped behind these two trucks. I studied the gap between them for a while and decided we could make it through the gap if we pulled in our large side mirrors.

We pulled the mirrors in to line up flush with the windows, crept up to the site of the accident, and pulled right through the gap left by the two trucks—with maybe no more than an inch or two to spare. Here is what was most interesting—after we drove through the gap, every car that had been sitting for hours followed us. We were now the lead car; no one else was on the interstate at that point because the highway had been shut down for so long.

This is how our drive went for the rest of that day. We were only able to drive about ten to twenty miles per hour, essentially on a sheet of ice. Then, we would come up on another accident scene, and we, as the lead car, would find another way to navigate through the maze of spun-out vehicles. In fact, sometimes traffic was so slow moving that our kids could hop out of the car, run into McDonald's off the highway, use the restroom, and run down the street a short distance and hop back into the van.

On another occasion, there were cars that had spun out and stalled all over the highway. We also sat at that scene for more than an hour. There was nothing anyone could do except wait for help. As our family studied the scene, we began thinking, "Wait, if we moved that car to the left, and then that car to the right, and then we could push that other car over to the side, we could get through."

I have no idea why no one else seemed to be thinking of ways to break free. It was as if everyone was content to be prisoners to the circumstances. All I knew is that with eight children, we were anxious to be home for Christmas. So, our family got out of the van and began pushing cars out of their stuck positions, or at least out of the way. Now, here is a great observation of human nature. As soon as we did that, other people in other cars came out to help us. There were over twenty people who had left their cars to come and help clear off the highway. Before we knew it, we had cleared a path on I-40, and everyone could pass through it again.

To make a long story short, we did not arrive home until 2:00 on Christmas morning. This should have been a seventeen-hour car ride. Instead, our journey took forty-two hours—forty-two hours of pure crazy! This story doesn't include the many times we prayed or the repeated times we spun out and did 360s in our fifteen-passenger van. But angels were with us, and we made it home safely.

We can glean many great lessons from this experience, not the least of which is the idea that most often, the anxious can perform well in a crisis. Anxious people understand that our purpose is to act, not to be acted upon. That concept can make a significant difference in the lives of many people.

Some of you may remember the great story of *The Wizard of Oz*. As you may recall, the Scarecrow needed a brain, the Tin Man needed a heart, and the Cowardly Lion needed courage. Ironically, throughout the movie, we see that it was actually the Scarecrow, the one who needed a brain, that came up with all the ideas. It was the Tin Man, the one who needed a heart, who was deeply connected to his own feelings and cared so much about others. And the Cowardly Lion, the one who supposedly lacked courage, was the bravest of them all.

Interestingly, the Cowardly Lion may have been afraid of everything, but he faced all of his fears head on. He was able to develop faith and courage, and overcome his fear through his journey. In fact, it was the Cowardly Lion's bravery that inspired his friends to be courageous as well. One author wrote, "The Cowardly Lion thinks he lacks courage, but he ultimately discovers that he had it within him all along. Sometimes we just need to look within ourselves to find the courage we need."[86]

Conclusion

Like the Cowardly Lion in *The Wizard of Oz*, those with anxiety often discover that they have more faith, hope, moxie, and grit than they ever imagined. These individuals can find hidden reservoirs of strength, fortitude, and stamina when they face a crisis or a challenge. To be with an anxious person in an emergency or crisis is to be with someone who has "been there and done that" and will help others navigate their way through such challenges. So, embrace your anxiety and prepare to help others through their crisis.

Questions for Thought

1. Do you know someone who is anxious but is actually good to have around in a crisis?
2. Have you ever surprised yourself by showing some competence and skill during an emergency?
3. Do you anticipate any obstacles and challenges that are coming soon in your life, and do you feel you know how to prepare for them?

SUPERPOWER 8

Being Healthy and Fit

It is a disgrace to grow old through sheer carelessness before seeing what manner of man you may become by developing your bodily strength and beauty to their highest limit.

—SOCRATES[87]

You know that feeling you get at the end of the holiday season when you are motivated to finally keep your New Year's resolution of eating healthier and working out more? Do you also remember how most of the time that motivation begins to ebb, and you eventually fall back to old habits, like eating junk food and forgetting to exercise? What if we told you that anxiety can catalyze the motivation for improved eating and working out so that your "new year, new me" inspiration never wears off? People with anxiety are more likely to be healthy and fit because of how important both factors are to maintaining their mental and physical health.

A wide body of research shows the impact that exercising and eating healthy can have on anxiety. Ironically, one of the main issues people with anxiety and depression struggle with is finding the motivation to exercise and eat right. In fact, there are many barriers associated with these practices, often causing people with anxiety to miss out on the amazing benefits of implementing physical activity and healthy foods into their daily lives. This chapter will first cover the benefits of working out and eating healthy for people with anxiety, then cover why these two factors can be hard for people with anxiety to implement. We will finish by discussing how to magnify the benefits and limit the negatives.

The Positive Relationship Between Working Out, Eating Healthy, and Anxiety

Research has shown that implementing physical activity and eating healthy in your daily routine can have major benefits on the bad symptoms of anxiety. An article written by staff members of the Mayo Clinic[88] says that regular exercise can have enough of an impact on anxiety symptoms to "make a big difference." A list of these benefits was compiled by Professor John J. Ratey in an article for *Harvard Health*[89] and includes the following:

- Engaging in exercise diverts you from the very thing you are anxious about.
- Moving your body decreases muscle tension, lowering the body's contribution to feeling anxious.
- Getting your heart rate up changes brain chemistry, increasing the availability of important anti-anxiety neurochemicals, including serotonin, gamma-aminobutyric acid (GABA), brain-derived neurotrophic factor (BDNF), and endocannabinoids.
- Exercise activates frontal regions of the brain responsible for executive function, which helps control the amygdala, our reacting system to real or imagined threats to our survival.
- Exercising regularly builds up resources that bolster resilience against stormy emotions.

These benefits were further expounded upon in a research paper published in the *Journal Frontiers of Psychiatry*, which found that the benefits listed above were "seen consistently across all age groups and racial/ethnic categories," showing that these benefits are truly universal in scope.[90]

Developing good eating habits can further alleviate anxiety symptoms. Researchers Nicholas G. Norwitz and Uma Naidoo found that "nutritional strategies aimed at addressing disturbances in metabolism and brain function can protect against anxiety disorders."[91] This finding was corroborated by a study called "Diet and Anxiety: A Scoping Review" in which researchers found that there was an association between "less anxiety and more fruits and vegetables, omega-3 fatty acids, 'healthy' dietary patterns, caloric restriction, breakfast consumption, ketogenic diet, broad-spectrum micronutrient supplementation, zinc, magnesium and selenium, probiotics, and a range of phytochemicals."[92]

We apologize for dumping all this research in your laps. But there is more! The Vanderbilt Medical Center released a simple infographic that shows which foods can help with bad anxiety symptoms. If you visit their website (vumc.org) and look up the article "Eat to Beat Anxiety,"[93] you can access this infographic showing good foods to eat to beat bad anxiety symptoms.

We hope you can truly see how beneficial being physically active and eating well can counteract the bad symptoms of anxiety. Brayden shares the following experience regarding how impactful being physically active is for him.

> I don't think I would have been able to get through either of my experiences with extreme anxiety if I couldn't exercise at the gym. Being physically active has always been a priority; however, it took on a new meaning when it became the only outlet I had to feel normal during my periods of extreme anxiety. The gym became the only place I could go where I felt normal again, and I felt like my anxiety was not omnipresent. In the gym, I was able to think clearly for a while. I was able to be myself. I was able to give my mind a rest and push my body instead. The only thing that got me through some days was knowing I could go to the gym and gain a brief respite from the bad anxiety I was constantly feeling. I encourage you to find your "gym." It doesn't have to be working out; it can be playing a sport, going for a run, or doing any other activity that elevates your heart rate. But I promise you that whatever activity you choose, it will play an undeniable role in overcoming bad anxiety.

Likewise, Mark shared his experience with exercise:

> I now believe one of the key reasons I went into a full-blown anxiety/panic period of my life was that I reduced my exercise routine because of my busy schedule. With

frequent panic episodes, I found myself depleted of all energy. I literally did not know if I could even walk to my mailbox, or around the block. However, one day, I decided, "If I drop dead from walking, then so be it!" I decided to walk three miles to my office. I did feel a bit anxious, and I wondered throughout that walk if I would be able to complete it. However, I did make it, and that gave me the confidence to continue this practice. Then, I began running again soon after this experience. First, one mile, and then eventually three miles. I was beginning to feel like my old self again. The more I exercised, the fewer anxiety symptoms I felt. This was twenty years ago. I continue to keep my exercise routine each day. As I begin my day with exercise, my anxiety symptoms have been minimized, or completely eradicated!

After reading about these positive benefits, you are probably wondering, why would people with anxiety not exercise and eat healthy? Sadly, this is a real issue that seems to be dichotomous in nature but that truly does impact people with anxiety and depression.

The Negative Side of Anxiety and Trying to Be Healthy and Fit

Our bad anxiety can have a negative impact on our desire to be physically active and eat well. Maryam Yvonne Marashi and her colleagues found that anxiety proved to be a barrier to many individuals when it came to engaging in physical activity.[94] While this study focused on participants within the framework of the COVID-19 pandemic, two different studies that had broader scopes and timeframes corroborated these results.[95] Researchers from both studies found that people with higher levels of anxiety and depression tend to be more sedentary and do less intense forms of physical activity.[96]

So, what gives? Why is exercise and eating healthy, two things that have been proven to help anxiety, so hard for people with anxiety to engage in? We believe that the easiest way to simplify this relationship is by asserting that bad anxiety can create tough mental and physical barriers in relation to exercise and eating healthy. A meta-analysis done by P. Gorczynski and colleagues summarizes this relationship perfectly:

> Many of the desirable outcomes of exercise for people with SMI (Severe Mental Illness), such as mood improvement, stress reduction and increased energy, are inversely related to the barriers of depression, stress and fatigue which frequently restrict their participation in exercise.[97]

For us personally, many of these barriers have been present. Brayden feels that the greatest barriers he faces when he is trying to be more physically active are fatigue, stress about a gym he's never been to, and worry regarding how people will view him at the gym. Mark's greatest barriers to working out are often managing a busy schedule and going to bed earlier so that he can wake up earlier and engage in a good exercise program.

We all have barriers. We all have excuses we can make to avoid working out and eating healthy. But if you have anxiety, this is something you can't make excuses to avoid. These two factors are too beneficial to avoid. These two components could potentially make all the difference in overcoming bad anxiety.

Magnifying the Good and Limiting the Bad

So, how can we, as anxious individuals, overcome the bad barriers we put up regarding exercise and eating healthily and truly embrace the great benefits provided by these two activities? We are glad you asked because we have some solutions that we feel will be game changers regarding the relationship between anxiety and exercise/eating healthy.

1. Find a way to overcome any barriers that you are placing in your mind regarding physical activity and eating well. A study done by Gordon J. G. Asmundson and colleagues advise the use of cognitive behavioral interventions (CBI) to aid in achieving long-term adherence to health-related goals.[98] CBIs are, essentially, procedures taught to an individual that focus on internal regulation of behavior.

This can be done by seeing a therapist, making yourself accountable to another person you trust, or using any other method that involves learning to regulate your internal narrative. Your internal narrative is what has created these barriers, so you need to come up with methods to overcome this negative internal narrative. We have found that once you overcome these barriers one time, it becomes easier and easier to overcome them until you barely even notice them. When you begin to see the benefits of exercise and eating healthy, your internal narrative becomes more positive until what were once barriers become speed boosts and catalysts that motivate you.

2. Start small and build over time. Many people who have made the decision to become healthier get overwhelmed. For better or worse, our world is inundated with articles, influencers, and companies who recommend a wide array of things that we need to do to become healthier. It is very easy to become overwhelmed by all of this. Start small. Start by setting a goal to go for a thirty-minute walk every day and maybe add one fruit or vegetable to your diet. Once this becomes easy, include some resistance training like doing a certain number of pushups every day on top of taking your thirty-minute walk and add another fruit or vegetable to your diet. The painter Vincent Van Gogh is known for saying, "Great things are done by a series of small things brought together."[99] This is exactly what you are doing. By taking small and simple steps, you can become physically active and eat healthy. Don't be overwhelmed by the weight of the challenge; just focus on the first step.

3. Find an accountability partner or someone who will go on this journey with you. Undertaking new changes is always easier if you have another person to lean on. The American Center for Disease Control and Prevention lists the following ideas for how you can include others to generate social support for the change you are attempting to make:

- Explain your interest in physical activity to friends and family. Ask them to support your efforts.
- Invite friends and family members to be physically active with you.
- Plan social activities involving physical activity.
- Develop new friendships with physically active people.
- Join a gym or group, such as the YMCA or a hiking club.[100]

By implementing these ideas, or any others you can identify, you can involve others in your journey. Who knows? Maybe you can help change another person's life along the way.

5. If you fail at some point, don't beat yourself up; try again tomorrow. Many people with anxiety have traits of perfectionism that can sabotage their plans and create a negative feedback loop if they fail at one aspect of their plan. However, this does not have to be the case. Indian guru and philosopher Osho is known for saying, "I love this world because it is imperfect. It is imperfect, and that's why it is growing; if it was perfect, it would have been dead. Growth is possible only if there is imperfection."[101] You are not perfect. You are not going to hit all your goals 100 percent of the time. And there is nothing wrong with that. Learn to enjoy your journey, the ups, and the downs. The only thing that matters is you keep trying, you keep growing, and you keep learning. Cultivate this mindset so that when perfectionistic thoughts try to drag you down, and when you inevitably fail to work out one time or eat unhealthy for a while, you can overcome these obstacles and give yourself some grace.

Conclusion

We hope this chapter has shown you how anxiety can catalyze your desire to become healthier. We understand that barriers can impede your desire to make the changes you need to become healthier. This does not need to be the case. If you follow the advice we have given you, we promise you that you will be able to reap the benefits of becoming healthier and your anxiety will become one of the greatest motivators for you to make and maintain this change.

Questions for Thought

1. Has your anxiety motivated you to be more conscious about your health?
2. Are any anxiety barriers keeping you from improving your eating and exercise habits?
3. What form of exercise do you find most beneficial in alleviating bad anxiety symptoms?

SUPERPOWER 9

Resilience, Grit, and Moxie

The only thing we have to fear is fear itself.
—FRANKLIN D. ROOSEVELT[102]

Most of us have heard the expression "when the going gets tough, the tough get going." However, it may be counterintuitive to realize that when the going gets tough, anxious individuals also get going! When faced with tough challenges, trials, or obstacles, the anxious person may surprise some because of their grit and stamina. Many of the anxious have faced the hardest challenges in life head on. The anxious can live by the mantra "I can do hard things" because they often do.

The great cowboy actor John Wayne once said, "Courage is being scared to death, but saddling up anyway."[103] There is an illusion that hard things are done by fearless people. However, this simply is not true. Many of the most heroic, brave acts have been done by those who are fearful and anxious. Yes, many incredible tasks have been done by those who have been scared to death, but they saddled up anyway!

What Is Resilience?

Resilience is "the process of adapting well in the face of adversity, trauma, tragedy, threats, or significant sources of stress."[104] Wendy Suzuki, author of *Good Anxiety: Harnessing the Power of the Most Misunderstood Emotion*, explained, "We need resilience every day to help us through challenges, disappointments, real and perceived insults, or any situation that might be painful. It's also one of the most important tools we have to draw from in the face of loss, sorrow, or trauma. . . . We rely on resilience all the time. And just as we are wired for survival, we are wired for resilience."[105]

Resilience is facing our trials and challenges head on.

Resilience is being afraid but moving forward with faith and confidence.

Resilience is not being defeated by harsh words, those who disagree with us, or those who do not like us.

Resilience is having strength and stamina to carry on, even when we do not think we can.

Resilience is sticking with our goal and plan, even when it becomes difficult.

Resilience is simply not quitting.

Some of you may be aware of Superbowl quarterback Steve Young. Many people may not know that Steve has suffered from anxiety throughout his life. Nevertheless, Steve had a fantastic high school athletic career. He was recruited by many colleges, but he chose to attend the same college his parents attended—Brigham Young University, named after Steve's great-great-great-grandfather.

Steve began his collegiate career as the eighth string quarterback on the football team. He was on the scout team, which means he ran the offense to prepare the first team defense for the upcoming game. He was getting beat up in every practice, his separation anxiety was getting the best of him, and at eighth string, he knew the possibilities of him ever playing were slim to none. On top of all this, the quarterback coach said he would never play a left-handed quarterback, and you guessed it, Steve was left-handed.

One night, at one of his lowest moments, Steve called his dad, nicknamed Grit, back home in Connecticut. He told his dad that football was not going well. Steve expressed that he wanted to quit and come home. Grit later said, "I thought, I don't want this kid to learn how to quit. . . . That is the worst thing in the world. I was determined to teach my kids how to not quit and see through the hard times."[106]

After Steve said, "Dad, I'm done. I'm quitting. I'm coming home," his dad responded, "You can certainly quit. But you can't come home. I'm not living with a quitter. So, you can decide for yourself."

Steve said, "I hung up mad. But I stayed at BYU."[107]

Steve was resilient. He stayed on the team. He worked harder than he ever had. Eventually, he became the second-string quarterback to All-American Jim MacMahon. When Jim left, Steve earned the starting job. Steve ultimately became a consensus All-American. He finished second in the Heisman Trophy voting, and he received the Davy O'Brien Award for the nation's most outstanding quarterback. Then he became the number-one pick in the NFL draft. Steve went on to play for fifteen seasons in the NFL. He was named the league's most valuable player in 1992 and 1994 and was the Super Bowl MVP in Super Bowl XXIX. Steve is a member of both the College Football Hall of Fame and the Pro Football Hall of Fame. Not bad for a guy who began his college career as the eighth-string quarterback![108]

Steve Young perfectly fits Wendy Suzuki's definition of resilience:

> So what is resilience?
> It's tenacity in response to falling short of your goal.
> It's courage to continue despite disappointment.
> It's the belief that you can and will do better if you put in the effort or practice.
> It's the confidence to believe that you matter.
> It's an openness to learning and relearning.
> It's the stamina to persevere.[109]

Steve's dad isn't named Grit for nothing. Steve epitomizes the grit that his father passed down to him. This grit is something each of us can possess. We can become resilient and gritty!

Saddling Up Despite Our Fears

Many of us have to face our fears and our inadequacies every day. But, as the saying goes, "That which doesn't kill us only makes us stronger." Author Holly Riordan wrote:

> You aren't a coward for feeling anxious in front of a crowd. Or when making a phone call. Or when answering an email. Or when doing any other activity that your friends

and family are able to do so easily, without breaking a sweat. You might be jealous of how naturally social interactions seem to come to everyone else, but you can't treat yourself like a punching bag. You aren't as cowardly as you feel. In fact, people with anxiety are some of the bravest humans out there.

You're brave for agreeing to future plans when you have no idea what your anxiety is going to be like that day. When there's no telling whether waking up and getting dressed will be simple that morning or whether it will feel like your throat is closing and your chest is on fire. You're brave for knowing there's a chance you're going to struggle, but deciding that you aren't going to let your anxiety get in the way of important opportunities. You're brave for realizing you're strong enough to endure. You've been through this before. You can go through it again. It isn't going to be easy, but none of your life has been easy, so you know you have what it takes to push through.

You're brave on the days when you show up with a racing pulse and shaking hands. When you keep going, even though your mind isn't making it easy for you. And you're brave on the days you stay in bed, too. On the days when you decide it would be bad for your mental health to leave the house and end up canceling plans even though it's the last thing you want to do. Making that decision is never easy. There's always a downside. Sure, staying home might lower your anxiety for a while, but you'll have to deal with people who are disappointed that you bailed—and your own disappointment about missing out on something that could have been fun.[110]

Mark shared the following example of being scared to death and saddling up anyway:

> I began my doctoral program at the age of thirty-four. Most other students in my program were in their late twenties and were quite academically gifted. I believe I got

accepted into my program by the skin of my teeth. I am sure that I qualified at the very base level of the academic requirements. I would often sit in graduate classes, listening to my professors and colleagues pontificate over philosophies and deep psychological principles. I would often think to myself, "What I am doing here?"

There were many reasons I felt I didn't belong. First of all, after reading five hundred pages of assigned journal articles for a class, I would think to myself, "I can barely understand anything I have read." Second, as we would discuss these articles in class, I would think, "I don't even know what my classmates are talking about, or my professors." Third, I was an average student in my undergraduate degree and in my master's program—not to even mention how poorly I did in high school. Fourth, I was married and had six children at the time. Most of my classmates did not have children, and most were not married. While many of them were studying or writing papers, I still had to be a husband and a father. I could make a list of all the reasons I should *not* have pursued a PhD, and most probably would have agreed with me. Despite all of these reasons for potential failure, I went to work and gave it full throttle.

Nevertheless, I went to work and gave it full throttle. I developed talents that I didn't realize I had. My capacity for completing herculean assignments grew. I developed the skill of researching and writing, and somehow, through God's grace, I passed all of my statistical classes. There must have been eight of us in our doctoral cohort, and I knew that I was the weakest link. However, I finished my dissertation before my colleagues and graduated before anyone else.

On the day that I completed my dissertation, one of my professors had to sign off on my project. We talked for a while, and then I said, "I cannot believe that I finished my dissertation before anyone else. We all knew that this program was like the Kentucky Derby, and I was the mule competing with thoroughbreds." I'll never forget my professor's response. He said, "It's just a reminder that the prizes do not always go to the brightest, or the most intellectually gifted, but to those who have grit, who are resilient, and who know how to do hard things." That may have been one of the greatest compliments I ever received. Despite my fears of not being able to complete a PhD, and despite my inadequacies, I was able to accomplish something I never dreamed I could do. I went on to become a professor at one of the most prestigious academic institutions in our country and continued to research and publish articles and books. Although I sometimes feel out of place when I rub shoulders with my Ivy League colleagues, I love the company my profession allows me to keep!

Many others have faced much more significant fears, like becoming a parent, battling a chronic illness, speaking in public, raising teenagers, dealing with a toxic person, going off to war, and taking care of an incapacitated family member. The list of fears is endless, but when the going gets tough, the anxious get going. In fact, those who are anxious can work miracles. They can accomplish tasks they may have never dreamed possible.

The Anxious Can Be Resilient

Once again, it seems counterintuitive that those who are anxious can have grit and be resilient, but it's true. If you are not fully convinced, let us share several reasons this is possible.

1. Anxiety often provides the energy, the drive, and the motivation to act. Although we previously used a similar example, consider the following scenario. If hundreds of people were relaxing on a beach and a large rogue wave was noticed off in the distance, those who possess some degree of anxiousness would not simply stand there to watch the wave crash upon all spectators. Instead, they would be the first ones to run in the opposite direction as fast as they could, hopefully taking a few people with them—like their kids! Therapist Kristine Tye explained,

> The energy that fuels anxious thoughts and behaviors is giving you what you need to take action and get unstuck. By not taking action, the energy is just getting bottled up inside you with nowhere to go but in circles. A mind spinning in circles or a body that fidgets or panics is stifling the energy of anxiety. Taking action can channel and alleviate that pressure, and the stress response can help you have the energy to do that.[111]

Anxiety and worry can be a catalyst for an individual taking action to avoid an undesirable outcome. In another study, researchers demonstrated that students and athletes who had anxiety symptoms actually had higher performance levels on tests and in their sports.[112] And speaking of sports, we have been surprised at how many exceptional professional athletes actually vomit before a game, match, or tournament because they are filled with anxiety. Surprisingly, most of these athletes go on to perform at the highest level during their games. Just because an individual has anxiety does not mean they cannot be resilient, or accomplish incredible feats, because they can and they do!

2. Anxiety can build your emotional resilience and help you develop grit. Dr. David H. Rosmarin, the author of *Thriving with Anxiety: 9 Tools to Make Your Anxiety Work for You*, wrote,

> Stress and anxiety . . . can help us recognize when we are running low on resources, thus serving as a helpful warning that allows us to rebalance before things get worse. Those who recalibrate in times of stress end up living healthier, stronger, more connected lives. Moreover, anxiety is an indication that we have a reservoir of inner strength to face adversity in the world, and it can thereby help us to lead and succeed.[113]

Without a doubt, stress and anxiety can build our resilience and help us to be strong in the face of challenges. The key, as Dr. Rosmarin suggested, is to recognize our anxiety, recalibrate in a time of crisis, and allow our challenges to make us stronger.

Often, those who have anxiety have suffered for a long time. They have been fearful of being in social situations, they have been scared to death to speak in public, they have worried themselves sick over issues in their families, and they have panicked over some of their physical symptoms that has made them think they are on the verge of death. Combine that with feeling nervous, jittery, unstable, unable to breathe, having a racing heart, and 101 other symptoms—this makes for an exceedingly difficult existence. However, most people with these symptoms still face life head on. They go to school and work, interact with others, give public speeches, run marathons, and even calm others down who are in a state of panic.

One of the most common treatments for anxiety is exposure therapy. This type of treatment involves facing our fears head on. Harvard Medical School professor Dr. David Rosmarin wrote, "With the help of a therapist, individuals with phobias to anything from snakes or spiders, to heights or medical procedures, gradually encounter that which makes them anxious. As they exercise their emotional strength—voluntarily and courageously—they become desensitized to their anxiety, and its effects decrease. . . . Anxiety can provide opportunities to flex our neural and emotional muscles, developing greater mental capacity to face day-to-day stressors more effectively."[114]

By doing difficult things every day, and by facing their fears, the anxious person builds a reservoir of strength, grit, courage, and stamina. Often, the suffering we experience from anxiety drives us to want to find solutions to our problems, overcome our fears, and learn techniques to deal with our worries and fears. Mark shared the following experience of how this happened in his life:

> Yes, there was a time in my life where I was burning the candle at both ends. I had major responsibilities at my work and was putting in more hours than I probably should have. I also had a significant ecclesiastical position in my church that demanded much of my time. Combining all of this with having eight children, some financial strains, and several other problems, I was at the end of my rope.
>
> I began to feel anxiety symptoms almost every day that eventually morphed into full-blown panic attacks. My wife

and I drove to the emergency room several times because I felt I was having a heart attack. For those who have done this drill before, you will understand that the doctors could never find anything wrong.

Finally, I began to take matters into my own hands because I was feeling so horrible. Every day I was literally cold and shaking, jittery, unstable, and in a state of panic. I diagnosed myself with generalized anxiety and began treating myself. Because of my busy schedule, I had stopped exercising, eating right, and getting enough sleep. I had also become laxed in my daily spiritual practices. I began my spiritual routines again and exercised, ate right, and enjoyed time with my family. My anxiety began to dissipate drastically, and life returned back to normal (whatever normal is!).

As I began to manage my life better, I learned that I could handle more. In truth, my life did not become less busy—it actually became busier than ever. However, by implementing healthy lifestyle practices, I can now handle more than I ever dreamed possible. That does not mean that life is easy, but I am able to manage the significant load that I carry.

To build resilience and grit, each of us will have to do hard things. Muscles grow when they are used and even break down to some degree when you work out. Likewise, as we face our anxieties, we too can develop the resilience and coping muscles that can help us become stronger, more confident, and even more capable. We know many individuals who have struggled with anxiety for years, and now the very things that paralyzed them with fear can be done with ease. Some of these individuals are both competent and confident; they speak in public; they can work a room (socially) with ease; they are not flattened by the events of the world; they are not overwhelmed by their insane schedules; and they are no longer discouraged by some of the trials and challenges they face.

3. The adversity and hardships we face help us overcome our fears and anxiety, and, in turn, become more resilient. Put another way, adversity can be a breeding ground for resiliency. No trial or hardship is wasted if it helps us become stronger, grittier, and more resilient. If we face difficult circumstances and we choose to curl up in the fetal position, lay under our covers, and be spoon fed tapioca pudding by our mothers, of course we will never develop grit or stamina. However, if we face those challenges head on, if we are scared to death but choose to saddle up anyway, then we will develop resiliency the same way we would exercise a muscle. The tearing down of the muscle fibers allows the muscle to grow back stronger than before.

Each time we face our fears, every time we confront a challenge, each time we do something hard or difficult, we are building our resilience. Wendy Suzuki wrote:

> When we challenge ourselves and grow more confident, we build our resilience. When we figure out how to dial down our body's stress response through relaxation techniques, we build our resilience. When we eat right, get enough sleep, and exercise, we boost our physical resilience and in turn, support our psychological resilience. . . . Actually, dear readers, resilience is full circle to *one of the most powerful* abilities that everyday anxiety affords us: the power to build our own personal and replenishable source of resilience in our lives. Anxiety helps build up our resilience stores: anxiety also alerts us to the need for recovery and self-care.[115]

The American Psychological Association made these recommendations to build resilience:

- **Prioritize relationships**, especially those who can validate your feelings.
- **Join a group**, to both receive support and give support to others.
- **Take care of your body**, focusing on proper nutrition, exercise, and sleep.
- **Practice mindfulness**, including yoga, prayer, meditation, and journaling.
- **Avoid negative outlets**, such as alcohol, drugs, or other substances.

- **Help others** and gain a sense of purpose.
- **Be proactive** in solving your problems.
- **Move towards your goals**, and work on them constantly.
- **Look for opportunities of self-discovery** as you determine what you have learned through the process.
- **Keep things in perspective** and identify areas of irrational thinking.
- **Accept that change is part of life**. Learn to be flexible.
- **Maintain a hopeful outlook**. An optimistic outlook will empower you.
- **Learn from the past** as you connect with what you have learned through previous experiences.[116]

Conclusion

Those who are anxious are not wimps or lightweights. They possess grit, discipline, and a strong, powerful work ethic. These anxious individuals can get things done; they make things happen; they are proactive instead of reactive. Re-evaluate your own anxiety and learn to identify and cultivate your own grit and perseverance. We know that it is in you!

Questions for Thought

1. What are three of the most difficult challenges you have faced in your life?
2. How do you feel that you handled those challenges?
3. How can you turn your anxiety into resilience?

SUPERPOWER 10

Becoming Your Best Self

*We are what we repeatedly do.
Excellence, then, is not an act, but a habit.*

—ARISTOTLE[117]

As we've mentioned throughout this book, anxiety is a true catalyst for becoming a better person across a variety of spectrums. This chapter is the culminating superpower of this assertion: that anxiety can motivate you to become the best version of yourself. In this chapter we will cover how this is the case and introduce a powerful tool known as cognitive reframing that can aid in viewing anxiety as a major benefit in your life.

What Is Cognitive Reframing?

Cognitive Reframing is a psychological technique that can aid you in viewing your anxiety as a positive motivating factor in your life. In the book *The Wiley Handbook of Cognitive Behavioral Therapy,* author David Clark defines cognitive reframing as "a technique used to shift your mindset so you're able to look at a situation, person, or relationship from a slightly different perspective."[118] There are many benefits to this technique, with psychotherapist Amy Morin stating that cognitive reframing can help you change your point of view to be more positive about problems, validate your emotions, and increase levels of compassion.[119] Not only does this technique have a wide variety of application, but research has also shown that it works. In an article about cognitive reframing, Dr. Seth Gillihan provided a literature review that showed successful research regarding the application of cognitive reframing in scenarios of depression, anxiety, PTSD, substance abuse disorders, lifestyle changes, and stress.[120]

So, how does this technique apply to the superpower of becoming the best version of yourself? Brayden shares the following story about how crucial cognitive reframing was to his mindset shift regarding his anxiety.

> It wasn't until I had my second major anxiety event that I began to take cognitive reframing seriously. Up until that point, I hadn't really tried to regulate my thoughts regarding my perception of anxiety and how it impacted me. I thought it was too hard of a change, and after my first major anxiety event, I thought I was permanently programmed to think of my anxiety as a problem I'd have to learn to deal with for the rest of my life. However, after a few sessions with my therapist, I was able to change my perception. Over the course of these sessions, my therapist told me about the research regarding how many thoughts we have a day and how many of those thoughts are negative. He also informed me that our brains are malleable and able to change; we just need to put the effort in to make those changes. We started working on cognitive reframing, and although it was hard at first, I began to see the benefits it provided. One technique we tried was daily affirmations to make positive thinking a more prominent factor in my life. Another technique we implemented was whenever I had a negative thought, I would immediately refute it and replace it with a rational or positive thought. While these techniques were difficult at first, I slowly began to reframe my thought process, and the benefits were astounding. Interestingly, my thoughts regarding my anxiety began to change as well. I began to see my anxiety as a major benefit in my life that helped motivate me to be better in every facet of my life. And the crazy thing is, that wasn't even the main goal of the cognitive reframing! I was just trying to be more positive about life in general,

and this revelation regarding my anxiety almost seemed like a happy byproduct. However, byproduct or not, this new outlook regarding anxiety allowed me to see the good it did in my life instead of focusing on the bad. Yes, anxiety can be hard. Yes, anxiety can make life difficult. Yes, anxiety can feel like a burden weighing your life down. However, there is so much more to it. Can anxiety help you become a better version of yourself? Yes! Can anxiety help you improve your relationships with others and become a more loving brother, sister, aunt, uncle, mom, dad, etc.? Yes! Can anxiety help you excel in the workplace? Yes! There is so much good your anxiety can do, and reframing how you look at your anxiety can be a major game changer. Take it from someone who has had anxiety so bad I couldn't get out of bed without my mom or dad getting me up and who has thought of ending his life because I believed the pain of anxiety was too great. I am here to say that anxiety has become one of the greatest benefits and aids in helping me become the best version of myself.

Now that we have addressed what cognitive reframing is, we will discuss how it can be used when applied specifically to anxiety.

Applying Cognitive Reframing to Anxiety

There are many techniques for cognitive reframing that can promote a better understanding of, and appreciation for, anxiety. Brayden has already listed two techniques above: affirmations and thought disputing. These techniques are great at refuting our own cognitive distortions. Sarah Fletcher, chief clinical officer of Sandstone Care, defines cognitive distortions as "thought patterns that cause a person to view reality in inaccurate and commonly negative ways."[121] Some examples of cognitive distortions include overgeneralization, catastrophizing, jumping to conclusions, magnification, personalization, and all-or-nothing thinking. We have all had these thought patterns. However, when they are reinforced through rumination, they can be detrimental. Fletcher lists five steps we need to follow to address cognitive distortions:

1. Write down the upsetting situation.
2. Identify upsetting feelings associated with the situation. It can be helpful to focus on one of the main feelings: fear, anxiety, sadness, depression, guilt, shame, and anger.
3. Identify your thoughts about the situation that are underlying the feelings. Questions can include . . .
    a. What bad thing do I expect to happen?
    b. What is missing in my life?
    c. What bad thing have I done?
4. Evaluation. Look at the situation and the accuracy of the upsetting thought.
5. Decide on the accuracy of your thought based on the evidence from step four. It is helpful to base your decision on evidence that is objective and based on facts rather than your beliefs or feelings.[122]

While this might seem like a lot to do, the more often you do it, the better you'll get at it and the quicker the process will be. These steps can be a major help in rewriting prominent cognitive distortions you have in your life.

If you are looking to simply improve your overall outlook on life and remove the negative thought patterns you have been stuck in, the technique of affirmations and disputing (challenging negative thoughts we have) can be very helpful. A 2020 study found that humans, on average, have more than 6,200 thoughts a day, with the majority of those thoughts being negative.[123] That means you have, on average, 6,200 chances to think positively throughout the day. However, research shows we are doing the opposite. Practicing daily affirmations and disputing thoughts can help change this ratio so that the majority of those 6,200 thoughts are positive and beneficial. Essentially, you are using these techniques to rewire your brain. This is a crazy concept to think about, but it's true! This ability is made possible through neuroplasticity. Neuroplasticity is defined in many ways, but the definition we will use for this book is "the ability of the brain to change in structure or function in response to experience."[124]

The experiences your brain is responding to are affirmations you are expressing and disputing the negative thought processes. Essentially, your brain is like a computer processing system. The system operates in accordance with the input that is provided. Once that input changes, the operation of the processing system will change along with it.

Now, why throw all this science at you and overemphasize the point that you can rewire your brain? Because we want you to see that you can go from viewing anxiety as a hindrance, and having it function as the filter that you see everything through, to ultimately seeing anxiety as a blessing that grants you superpowers. This shift may not be easy and may involve utilizing the techniques mentioned above, but it *is* possible.

How Anxiety Can Help You Become the Best Version of Yourself

Your anxiety is your own version of Superman's strength or Spider-Man's web-slinging. It has the capacity to differentiate you from everyone else in a positive way, much like how these superheroes' powers do the same for them. You have been granted a gift that, when channeled correctly, can lead you to heights you never would have been able to reach without it. In this section we will lay out some reasons anxiety can motivate you to be the best version of yourself.

Reason 1: Few have been blessed with this gift—and that's a good thing. While it seems everyone nowadays has some form of anxiety, our numbers are relatively few. Studies show that roughly 6.8 million Americans, or 3.1 percent of the population, have been diagnosed with generalized anxiety disorder (GAD).[125] Extrapolate those numbers to the rest of the world, and we could conclude that we don't make up a large percentage of the population. Now, utilizing a positive mindset and positive cognitive reframing, we can view this as a benefit for individuals diagnosed with GAD. In our minds, this means few of us have this superpower of anxiety. Most people don't have this amazing catalyst for development that we do. We have provided you with evidence throughout this chapter regarding how anxiety can have benefits on mental, emotional, and physical factors. This evidence speaks to one overlying fact: Anxiety can help you become the best version of yourself, and you are part of the lucky few who have been blessed with this gift.

Reason 2: In a world that is seeing increasing levels of anxiety, we are uniquely prepared to thrive. The COVID-19 pandemic was a watershed moment for increased levels of anxiety across the world, and since then, cases of anxiety have been rising.[126] In an environment where anxiety is becoming more and more prevalent, those of us who have been dealing with anxiety for years are uniquely positioned to thrive. It's like those of us with anxiety are fish and the world just lost most of its landmass and became purely ocean. While other species are trying to adapt to this new environment, we as fish are not only already equipped to survive, but the growth of our habitat also means we can expand and thrive.

Reason 3: Anxiety truly is a motivator. We have been calling anxiety a motivator—or as Brayden likes to call it, "nature's pre-workout,"—this entire chapter, but it truly can motivate us to become the best version of ourselves. In an article for the BBC titled "How to Use Anxiety to Your Advantage," Tracy Dennis-Tiwary addressed anxiety as a motivator:

> When we're anxious, not only are we more creative and innovative, but our brains respond with greater focus and efficiency when we face the unpredictable. Anxiety is thus more than the "fear circuitry" of the brain. Anxiety also activates our drives for reward and social connection, impelling us to work for what we care about, connect with others, and be more productive. That's why, from the perspective of evolutionary theory, anxiety isn't destructive. Anxiety embodies the logic of survival.[127]

We love the phrase "anxiety embodies the logic of survival" because, at the end of the day, anxiety truly motivates us to survive and become the best version of ourselves.

Reason 4: If you utilize cognitive reframing for anxiety, there is little you can't achieve. For many of us, anxiety presents the greatest barrier to our development as a person. If you can reframe that and change anxiety from being the greatest barrier to the greatest motivator, the sky is the limit for what you can achieve. Brayden shared this insight:

> When I first began to deal with anxiety, I quickly came to believe that it was the greatest hindrance to my success. Everything I did, every decision I made, was framed within the context of how my anxiety would react to the situation. However, after I began to change my outlook on anxiety and see it as more of a benefit, my whole mental landscape changed. Now, I look at situations and think, "How is my anxiety going to help me?" My greatest weakness has become one of my greatest strengths, and it is much easier for me to make changes in my life now that I have my anxiety as a partner rather than an enemy. Now, when I am about to make a change or improvement in my life that might be hard to implement, I simply think, "This can't be harder than learning to see my perceived greatest weakness as a strength. I can do this." In this way, cognitive reframing and changing my overall perception of anxiety has allowed me to thrive in ways I never thought possible.

Your greatest weakness can become your greatest strength. Once you realize that and do the work to make it true, the sky is the limit for who you can become and what you can accomplish.

Conclusion

In this chapter, we have endeavored to show you how anxiety can motivate you to become the best version of yourself. Utilizing techniques such as cognitive reframing can help you see your anxiety not as a weakness but as a prime motivator for good in your life. We believe anxiety is a superpower. We believe that it can motivate you better than almost anything else. We believe that you can be great *with* your anxiety.

Questions for Thought

1. Have you ever done cognitive reframing?
2. How has your anxiety allowed you to become the best version of yourself?
3. What is one change you are going to make regarding how you view your anxiety?

CONCLUSION

A Little Inconvenience

*Anxiety can be good . . . or bad.
It turns out that it is really up to you.*

—DR. WENDY SUZUKI[128]

Perhaps some of you have heard the following couplet: "Two men looked out from prison bars, one saw the mud, the other saw stars."[129] Life seems to boil down to how we view the experiences we encounter each day. Of course, we can view our life experiences positively or negatively. Mark and Dr. Ted Asay wrote:

> By figuratively looking up, focusing on the positive, and ignoring the negative, we can improve our lives and increase our overall wellbeing and quality of life. As mental health professionals, we have come to understand that an individual's quality of life is often determined by what they choose to focus on. In fact, it seems that a happy life boils down to focusing on the cheerful, healthy, and positive experiences that surround us.[130]

Furthermore, we can view our own anxiety as a stumbling block or a stepping stone. Ultimately, how we perceive our anxiety, and respond to it, is up to each of us. We believe that we are not here on this earth to be victims. We are here to act, not to be acted upon.

Years ago, Mark was meeting with an executive for a consulting company in the Dallas area. This man was highly successful in the corporate world. However, Mark was aware that this individual battled bipolar disorder. One day, Mark asked, "How do you do it? You are running this successful company, you have a crazy schedule, there are many things on your plate, and yet, you battle bipolar disorder every day. I know people who suffer from this illness, and they cannot even get out of bed some days."

This man simply responded, "Each day, I make a choice. I decide I am going to run bipolar disorder; I will not let this illness run me."

A profound response. We can either be victims to our anxiety, or we can embrace it, learn from it, manage it, and run our lives. We do not have to be hindered or crippled by anxiety! We hope that as you have read this book, you have become aware of some of the benefits of being anxious. Anxiety does not have to be a curse or a life sentence to the rock pile. Once again, how you view your anxiety and respond to it will make a huge difference in the quality of your life.

Years ago, a made-for-television movie titled *Just a Little Inconvenience* aired during prime time. The movie was about a Vietnam war veteran, Kenny Briggs, who had lost both an arm and a leg in the war. Briggs learned to become a skilled snow skier, despite being a double amputee. In one scene, someone asks Briggs how he can ski so well with his profound handicaps. Briggs responds that his condition is not a handicap but "just a little inconvenience."[131] What an incredible reframe! Briggs chose not to let his ailment define him. Instead, he chose to view his catastrophic injury as "a little inconvenience." This is an amazing response, and we can all learn something from it.

Consider your anxiety as "a little inconvenience." An inconvenience does not need to alter your life drastically or ruin your goals and dreams. Furthermore, with that inconvenience, you can learn wonderful life lessons; you can become a better version of yourself, and you can help others along the way.

Moreover, no one lives a perfect life. We all have problems. Every human that we know struggles with something. Author, speaker, and columnist Regina Brett said, "If we all threw our problems in a pile and saw everyone else's, we'd grab ours back."[132] How true! We know of some who struggle with divorce, disease, death, illness, financial catastrophes, toxic relationships, and an assortment of other huge issues. Maybe struggling with anxiety isn't all that bad. In fact, in dealing with this ailment, maybe this is how we can become stronger, full of faith and hope, and even more confident.

Anxiety Superpowers

We have discussed the following anxiety superpowers:

1. High levels of motivation
2. Empathy, care, and concern
3. Spidey sense
4. An analytical mind
5. Nurturing leadership
6. Self-awareness
7. Emergency preparedness
8. Being healthy and physically fit
9. Resilience, grit, and moxie
10. Becoming your best self

We want to emphasize that this is not an all-inclusive list. Perhaps there are hundreds of other benefits to being anxious. Every weakness that anxiety seems to bring with it can become a strength if we deliberately work on that issue. We encourage you to choose one of the traits we have mentioned in this book and deliberately work on it for a week or two, or perhaps even a couple of months. When you feel confident in that skill or strength, work on another one. Perhaps there are traits, skills, and abilities that we have not mentioned in this book that you would like to work on. What are you waiting for? Go for it! Write down your goals and plan on a 3x5 card, or on the notepad of your phone or tablet, and review your goals and plan multiple times each day. Then go to work!

The most important area of your life to improve upon is the one you are having the most difficult time with.[133] If you really want to become happier, more confident, and pleasant to be around, identify your weakest link and go to work on it.[134] With divine help, your weakness can become a strength. For example, if you live your life through the lens of fear, you will most likely feel anxiety symptoms every day. But what if you changed the way you thought about fear? What if instead of viewing everything through the lens of fear, you decided to view things through the lens of love or compassion? When your children make a mistake, instead of fearing that the next step for them is prison or reform school, what if you changed the way you view your children? If you view them through the lens of love, you will feel gratitude for having the children that you have. You would see every day you have with them as a blessing. You would remember the mistakes that you made as a child and realize that you turned out pretty good. You would have the faith that your children are probably going to turn out to be pretty good people.

Likewise, instead of viewing the world through the lens of fear, what if you changed your view and you saw things through the lens of faith? Instead of expecting the worst possible outcomes in every scenario, you could expect the best, or even average, outcomes. Instead of viewing everything as a crisis or catastrophe, you would have the awareness that most things work out. You could begin to see all of the wonderful beauties in life. You would relish your time spent in nature. You would savor the moments you have together with those you love the most. You would become more aware of the small miracles that surround you every day. Instead of being angry that your car ran out of gas, you could be grateful that there is a gas station just a few hundred feet down the street. Instead of being frustrated that you never seem to get ahead financially, you could be happy that you have a roof over your head, plenty of food to eat, and a warm place to gather with loved ones on a cold winter's night.

Viewed in a healthy way, your anxiety can become one of the great blessings in your life. Anxiety is not weakness. To be anxious is to be aware—perhaps too aware—of what is around us. Your anxiety can be the catalyst to help you become a better person, to achieve your goals and dreams, and to lift and build those around you.

We encourage you to go forward with faith. Go after your goals and dreams. Don't let anything stand in your way. Remember, anxiety is not a great handicap. It's just a little inconvenience. You've got this!

ENDNOTES

1. PsychCentral. Quotes about anxiety. Retrieved July 23, 2024, from https://psychcentral.com/anxiety/quotes-about-anxiety#quotes-on-anxiety
2. Corrie ten Boom. PsychCentral. (n.d.). Quotes about anxiety. Retrieved July 5, 2024, from https://psychcentral.com/anxiety/quotes-about-anxiety#living-with-anxiety
3. Robert Tew. Today. Anxiety quotes. Retrieved May 5, 2024, from https://www.today.com/life/quotes/anxiety-quotes-rcna126836
4. PsychCentral. (n.d.). 45 quotes about anxiety. Retrieved February 24, 2024, from https://psychcentral.com/anxiety/quotes-about-anxiety
5. Anxiety and Depression Association of America. (n.d.). Anxiety disorders—Facts and statistics. Retrieved February 24, 2024, from https://adaa.org/understanding-anxiety/facts-statistics
6. Harvard Medical School. (2007). National Comorbidity Survey (NCS). Data Table 1: Lifetime prevalence DSM-IV/WMH-CIDI disorders by sex and cohort. Retrieved August 21, 2017, from https://www.hcp.med.harvard.edu/ncs/index.php
7. Summit Malibu. (n.d.). 9 famous people and celebrities with anxiety disorders. Retrieved February 20, 2024, from https://summitmalibu.com/blog/9-famous-people-and-celebrities-with-anxiety-disorders/
8. Wikipedia. (n.d.). List of people with an anxiety disorder. Retrieved February 24, 2024, from https://en.wikipedia.org/wiki/List_of_people_with_an_anxiety_disorder
9. Aarons-Mele, M. (n.d.). How history's greatest leaders managed anxiety & fear. LinkedIn. Retrieved February 24, 2024, from https://www.linkedin.com/pulse/how-historys-greatest-leaders-managed-anxiety-fear-morra-aarons-mele/
10. Hardy, L., & Hutchinson, A. (2007). Effects of performance anxiety on effort and performance in rock climbing: A test of processing efficiency theory. Anxiety, Stress, & Coping, 20(2), 147-161. https://doi.org/10.1080/10615800701217035
11. Tye, K. (n.d.). 7 ways anxiety actually works to your advantage. Good Therapy. Retrieved February 20, 2024, from https://www.goodtherapy.org/blog/7-ways-anxiety-actually-works-to-your-advantage-0202165
12. Davey, G. C. L., Tallis, F., & Capuzzo, N. (1996). Beliefs about the consequences of worrying. *Cognitive Therapy and Research, 20,* 499–520.
13. Hebert, E. A., Dugas, M. J., Tulloch, T. G., & Holowka, D. W. (2014). Positive beliefs about worry: A psychometric evaluation of the Why Worry-II. *Personality and Individual Differences, 56,* 3–8.
14. Sweeny, K., & Dooley, M. D. (2017). The surprising upsides of worry. Social and Personality Psychology Compass, 11, Article e12311. https://doi.org/10.1111/spc3.12311
15. McCaul, K. D., Branstetter, A. D., O'Donnell, S. M., Jacobson, K., & Quinlan, K. B. (1998). A descriptive study of breast cancer worry. *Journal of Behavioral Medicine, 21,* 565–579.
16. Frijda, N. H., Kuipers, P., & ter Schure, E. (1989). Relations among emotion, appraisal, and emotion action readiness. *Journal of Personality and Social Psychology,* 57, 212–228.
17. Sweeny & Dooley. (2017). 4.
18. Bassett, L. (2001). *From Panic to Power: Proven Techniques to Calm Your Anxieties, Conquer Your Fears, and Put You in Control of Your Life.* HarperCollins, 25.
19. Ibid., 3.

20. Wilding, M. (2021, June 28). 14 traits of highly sensitive people. *Psychology Today.* https://www.psychologytoday.com/us/blog/trust-yourself/202106/14-traits-of-highly-sensitive-people
21. Folk, J. (2021, May 18). Hypersensitive, super sensitive nerves, senses—anxiety symptoms. Anxietycentre.com. https://www.anxietycentre.com/anxiety-disorders/symptoms/hypersensitivity/
22. Tibi-Elhanany, Y., & Shamay-Tsoory, S. G. (2011). Social cognition in social anxiety: First evidence for increased empathic abilities. *Israel Journal of Psychiatry and Related Sciences, 48(2),* 98–106.
23. Merriam-Webster. (n.d.). Compassion. In Merriam-Webster.com dictionary. Retrieved April 3, 2024, from https://www.merriam-webster.com/dictionary/compassion
24. PsychCentral. (n.d.). Quotes about anxiety. Retrieved February 17, 2025, from https://psychcentral.com/anxiety/quotes-about-anxiety
25. George, L., & Stopa, L. (2008). Private and public self-awareness in social anxiety. *Journal of Behavior Therapy and Experimental Psychiatry, 39(1),* 57–72. https://doi.org/10.1016/j.jbtep.2006.09.004
26. Gilboa-Schechtman, E., Foa, E. B., & Amir, N. (1999). Attentional biases for facial expressions in social phobia: The face-in-the-crowd paradigm. *Cognition and Emotion, 13,* 305–318.
27. Beckner, V. L. (2023, October 2). Anxiety gets a bad rap: Understand your healthy alarm system. Psychology Today. https://www.psychologytoday.com/us/blog/harnessing-principles-of-change/202104/anxiety-gets-bad-rap-understand-your-healthy-alarm
28. Barlow, D. H., & Ellard, K. K. (n.d.). Anxiety and related disorders. Noba. https://nobaproject.com/modules/anxiety-and-related-disorders
29. Familydoctor.org Editorial Staff. (2022, December 6). Generalized anxiety disorder. Familydoctor.org. https://familydoctor.org/condition/generalized-anxiety-disorder/
30. Bacon, F. (1597). *Meditationes Sacrae.* Excusum impensis Humfredi Hooper.
31. Anxiety gets a bad rap: Understand your healthy alarm system. Psychology Today. https://www.psychologytoday.com/us/blog/harnessing-principles-of-change/202104/anxiety-gets-bad-rap-understand-your-healthy-alarm.it.
32. LaFreniere, L. S., & Newman, M. G. (2020). Exposing worry's deceit: Percentage of untrue worries in generalized anxiety disorder treatment. *Behavior Therapy, 51(3),* 413–423. https://doi.org/10.1016/j.beth.2019.07.003
33. Goodreads. (n.d.). Marie Curie quotes. Retrieved May 13, 2024, from https://www.goodreads.com/quotes/16738-nothing-in-life-is-to-be-feared-it-is-only
34. Merriam-Webster. (n.d.-a). Analytic. In Merriam-Webster.com dictionary. Retrieved from https://www.merriam-webster.com/dictionary/analytic
35. Merriam-Webster. (n.d.-b). Analysis. In Merriam-Webster.com dictionary. Retrieved from https://www.merriam-webster.com/dictionary/analysis
36. Indeed. (n.d.). Analytical thinking vs. critical thinking (plus jobs that use them). Retrieved from https://www.indeed.com/career-advice/career-development/analytical-thinking-vs-critical-thinking
37. Marques, L. (2020, October 27). Do I have anxiety or worry: What's the difference? *Harvard Health.* https://www.health.harvard.edu/blog/do-i-have-anxiety-or-worry-whats-the-difference-2018072314303
38. Johns Hopkins Medicine. (2024, April 16). Generalized anxiety disorder (GAD). https://www.hopkinsmedicine.org/health/conditions-and-diseases/generalized-anxiety-disorder

ENDNOTES

39. Mayo Clinic. (2017, October 13). Generalized anxiety disorder. https://www.mayoclinic.org/diseases-conditions/generalized-anxiety-disorder/symptoms-causes/syc-20360803
40. Stein, M. (2023, October 9). Why you worry: Obsessing, overthinking, and overanalyzing explained. Anxiety Solutions of Denver. https://effectivetherapysolutions.com/anxiety/why-you-worry-obsessing-overthinking-and-overanalyzing-explained
41. Stern, V. (2024, February 20). Why we worry. *Scientific American.* https://www.scientificamerican.com/article/why-we-worry/
42. Zainal, N. H., & Newman, M. G. (2018). Worry amplifies theory-of-mind reasoning for negatively valanced social stimuli in generalized anxiety disorder. *Journal of Affective Disorders, 227,* 824–833. https://doi.org/10.1016/j.jad.2017.11.084
43. Pace, B. (n.d.). Understanding why we worry may help us stop doing it. Towson University. https://www.towson.edu/news/2020/tu-psychology-covid-worrying.html
44. Quintus Horatius Flaccus (Horace), Epistles, 1.2.40.
45. Doman, J. L. (2019, October 24). 8 traits of a highly analytical mind. Medium. https://joshldoman.medium.com/dissecting-the-mind-of-an-overthinker-be74948e6d7c
46. Doman, J. L. (2019, October 24).
47. Benjamin Franklin, Good Reads, accessed 13 February 2025; https://www.goodreads.com/quotes/10435396-do-not-anticipate-trouble-or-worry-about-what-may-never
48. Moosath, A. (2023, November 8). Anxiety can be turned into a leadership superpower: Morra Aarons-Mele. *Forbes India.* https://www.forbesindia.com/article/mentors-and-mavens/anxiety-can-be-turned-into-a-leadership-superpower-morra-aaronsmele/89555/1
49. Porter, J. (2014, January 28). Relax, being anxious makes you a good leader. Fast Company. https://www.fastcompany.com/3025488/relax-being-anxious-makes-you-a-good-leader
50. Aarons-Mele, M. (2023). *The anxious achiever: Turn your biggest fears into your leadership superpower.* Harvard Business Review Press. 21.
51. Suzuki, W., & Fitzpatrick, B. (2021). *Good anxiety: Harnessing the power of the most misunderstood emotion.* Atria Books. 146–147.
52. Suzuki, W. (2021). 147.
53. Aarons-Mele, M. (2020, May 11). Leading through anxiety. *Harvard Business Review.* https://hbr.org/2020/05/leading-through-anxiety
54. Anitha Moosath, "Anxiety Can Be Turned into a Leadership Superpower: Morra Aarons-Mele," Forbes India, 8 November 2023; https://www.forbesindia.com/article/mentors-and-mavens/anxiety-can-be-turned-into-a-leadership-superpower-morra-aaronsmele/89555/1
55. Morra Aarons-Mele, "Leading Through Anxiety," Harvard Business Review, 11 May 2020; https://hbr.org/2020/05/leading-through-anxiety
56. Beard, A. (2020, May 11). How history's great leaders managed anxiety. Harvard Business Review. https://hbr.org/2020/05/how-historys-great-leaders-managed-anxiety
57. Aarons-Mele, Morra. 2023. *The Anxious Achiever: Turn Your Biggest Fears into Your Leadership Superpower.* Harvard Business Review Press, 22.
58. Beard, Alison. (2020, May 11). "How History's Great Leaders Managed Anxiety," Harvard Business Review, https://hbr.org/2020/05/how-historys-great-leaders-managed-anxiety.
59. Buchanan, L. (2018, May 8). All leaders have anxiety. Here's how the best ones deal with it. Inc. https://www.inc.com/leigh-buchanan/anxiety-is-the-leaders-best-friend-and-worst-enemy.html
60. Morra Aarons-Mele, 2023, 21.

61. Goodreads. (n.d.). Aristotle quotes. Retrieved May 24, 2024, from https://www.goodreads.com/quotes/3102-knowing-yourself-is-the-beginning-of-all-wisdom
62. Merriam-Webster. (n.d.). Self-awareness. In Merriam-Webster.com dictionary. https://www.merriam-webster.com/dictionary/self-awareness
63. Eurich, T. (2023, April 6). What self-awareness really is (and how to cultivate it). *Harvard Business Review.* https://hbr.org/2018/01/what-self-awareness-really-is-and-how-to-cultivate-it
64. Eurich T. (2023, April 6)
65. Eurich T. (2023, April 6)
66. Well, T. (n.d.). Does self-awareness make you more anxious? *Psychology Today.* https://www.psychologytoday.com/us/blog/the-clarity/202109/does-self-awareness-make-you-more-anxious
67. Wang, Y., Chen, J., Zhang, X., Lin, X., Sun, Y., Wang, N., Wang, J., & Luo, F. (2022). The relationship between perfectionism and social anxiety: A moderated mediation model. *International Journal of Environmental Research and Public Health, 19(19),* 12934. https://doi.org/10.3390/ijerph191912934
68. Limburg, K., Watson, H. J., Hagger, M. S., & Egan, S. J. (2016). The relationship between perfectionism and psychopathology: A meta-analysis. *Journal of Clinical Psychology, 73(10),* 1301–1326. https://doi.org/10.1002/jclp.22435
69. UPMC Health Beat. (n.d.). How perfectionism is linked to anxiety and mental health. https://share.upmc.com/2021/05/perfectionism-linked-to-anxiety/
70. Eurich T. (2023, April 6)
71. Silvia, P. J., & O'Brien, M. E. (2004). Self-awareness and constructive functioning: Revisiting "The human dilemma." *Journal of Social and Clinical Psychology, 23(4),* 475–489. https://doi.org/10.1521/jscp.23.4.475.40307
72. Ridley, D. S., Schutz, P. A., Glanz, R. S., & Weinstein, C. E. (1992). Self-regulated learning: The interactive influence of metacognitive awareness and goal-setting. *The Journal of Experimental Education, 60(4),* 293–306. https://doi.org/10.1080/00220973.1992.9943867
73. Fletcher, C., & Bailey, C. (2003). Assessing self-awareness: Some issues and methods. *Journal of Managerial Psychology, 18(5),* 395–404. https://doi.org/10.1108/02683940310484008
74. Sutton, A., Williams, H. M., & Allinson, C. W. (2015). A longitudinal, mixed method evaluation of self-awareness training in the workplace. *European Journal of Training and Development, 39(7),* 610–627. https://doi.org/10.1108/ejtd-04-2015-0031
75. Silvia, P. J., & O'Brien, M. E. (2004).
76. Humber River Health. (2022, January 27). The benefits of self-awareness. Retrieved from https://www.hrh.ca/2022/01/27/the-benefits-of-self-awareness/
77. Vaish, A., Grossmann, T., & Woodward, A. (2008). Not all emotions are created equal: The negativity bias in social-emotional development. *Psychological Bulletin, 134(3),* 383–403. https://doi.org/10.1037/0033-2909.134.3.383
78. Goodreads. (n.d.). Lao Tzu quotes. Retrieved May 24, 2024, from https://www.goodreads.com/quotes/2979-knowing-others-is-intelligence-knowing-yourself-is-true-wisdom-mastering
79. Ronan, A. (2018, June 8). The upside of chronic anxiety: Being good in emergencies. The Guardian. https://www.theguardian.com/society/2018/jun/08/the-upside-of-chronic-anxiety-being-good-in-emergencies
80. Holland, J. R. (1980, March 18). For times of trouble. Brigham Young University Speeches. https://speeches.byu.edu/talks/jeffrey-r-holland/times-trouble/

81. El Zein, M., Wyart, V., & Grèzes, J. (2015). Anxiety dissociates the adaptive functions of sensory and motor response enhancements to social threats. eLife, 4, Article e10274. https://doi.org/10.7554/eLife.10274
82. Caron, C. (2023, June 22). The upside of anxiety. *New York Times.* https://www.nytimes.com/2022/01/19/well/mind/anxiety-benefits.html
83. Ronan, A. (2018)
84. Joyce, E. (2020, March 18). I shine in a crisis. Medium. https://medium.com/invisible-illness/i-shine-in-a-crisis-bd0490bff5d1
85. Friedlander, J. (2019, January 23). When bad circumstances make anxiety vanish. *Vice.* https://www.vice.com/en/article/9kp5p8/when-bad-circumstances-make-anxiety-vanish
86. Dwoskin, J. (2023, March 3). Lessons we can learn from the Cowardly Lion in *The Wizard of Oz* and how we can tap into our own courage. LinkedIn. https://www.linkedin.com/pulse/courageous-lessons-we-can-learn-from-cowardly-lion-wizard-dwoskin-/
87. Socrates. (n.d.). Goodreads. Retrieved June 22, 2024, from https://www.goodreads.com/author/quotes/275648.Socrates?page=10#:~:text=Socrates%20Quotes&text=Sometimes%20you%20have%20to%20lose,you%20come%20to%20your%20senses.&text=.%20.%20it%20is%20a%20disgrace,beauty%20to%20their%20highest%20limit
88. Mayo Foundation for Medical Education and Research. (2023, December 23). Depression and anxiety: Exercise eases symptoms. Mayo Clinic. https://www.mayoclinic.org/diseases-conditions/depression/in-depth/depression-and-exercise/art-20046495#:~:text=Regular%20exercise%20may%20improve%20depression,them%20over%20the%20long%20term
89. Ratey, J. J. (2019, October 24). Can exercise help treat anxiety? *Harvard Health.* https://www.health.harvard.edu/blog/can-exercise-help-treat-anxiety-2019102418096
90. Anderson, E., & Shivakumar, G. (2013). Effects of exercise and physical activity on anxiety. *Frontiers in Psychiatry, 4.* https://doi.org/10.3389/fpsyt.2013.00027
91. Norwitz, N. G., & Naidoo, U. (2021). Nutrition as metabolic treatment for anxiety. *Frontiers in Psychiatry, 12.* https://doi.org/10.3389/fpsyt.2021.598119
92. Aucoin, M., LaChance, L., Naidoo, U., Remy, D., Shekdar, T., Sayar, N., Cardozo, V., Rawana, T., Chan, I., & Cooley, K. (2021). Diet and anxiety: A scoping review. *Nutrients, 13(12),* 4418. https://doi.org/10.3390/nu13124418
93. Plus, H. (n.d.). Eat to beat anxiety. Eat to Beat Anxiety | Vanderbilt Faculty & Staff Health and Wellness. https://www.vumc.org/health-wellness/resource-articles/eat-beat-anxiety
94. Marashi, M. Y., Nicholson, E., Ogrodnik, M., Fenesi, B., & Heisz, J. J. (2021). A mental health paradox: Mental health was both a motivator and barrier to physical activity during the COVID-19 pandemic. *PLOS ONE, 16(4).* https://doi.org/10.1371/journal.pone.0239244
95. Song, M. R., Lee, Y., Baek, J., & Miller, M. (2011). Physical activity status in adults with depression in the National Health and Nutrition Examination Survey, 2005–2006. *Public Health Nursing, 29(3),* 208–217. https://doi.org/10.1111/j.1525-1446.2011.00986.x
96. Helgadóttir, B., Forsell, Y., & Ekblom, Ö. (2015). Physical activity patterns of people affected by depressive and anxiety disorders as measured by accelerometers: A cross-sectional study. *PLOS ONE, 10(1).* https://doi.org/10.1371/journal.pone.0115894
97. Firth, J., Rosenbaum, S., Stubbs, B., Gorczynski, P., Yung, A. R., & Vancampfort, D. (2016). Motivating factors and barriers towards exercise in severe mental illness:

ENDNOTES

98. A systematic review and meta-analysis. *Psychological Medicine, 46(14),* 2869–2881. https://doi.org/10.1017/s0033291716001732 and barriers towards exercise in severe mental illness: A systematic review and meta-analysis. *Psychological Medicine, 46(14),* 2869–2881. https://doi.org/10.1017/s0033291716001732
98. Mason, J. E., Faller, Y. N., LeBouthillier, D. M., & Asmundson, G. J. G. (2019). Exercise anxiety: A qualitative analysis of the barriers, facilitators, and psychological processes underlying exercise participation for people with anxiety-related disorders. *Mental Health and Physical Activity, 16,* 128–139. https://doi.org/10.1016/j.mhpa.2018.11.003
99. Person, & Garcia, E. (2023, August 14). Unveiling 8 inspiring quotes from Vincent van Gogh. *1st Handmade Portraits and Reproductions.* https://www.1st-art-gallery.com/article/captivating-wisdom-from-vincent-van-gogh/
100. Centers for Disease Control and Prevention. (n.d.). Overcoming barriers to physical activity. Centers for Disease Control and Prevention. https://www.cdc.gov/physical-activity-basics/overcoming-barriers/index.html#:~:text=Make%20physical%20activity%20a%20regular,an%20exercise%20group%20or%20class
101. Osho. (n.d.). Goodreads. Retrieved June 22, 2024, from https://www.goodreads.com/quotes/172982-i-love-this-world-because-it-is-imperfect-it-is
102. As cited in The White House, Franklin D. Roosevelt, the 32nd President of the United States. https://www.whitehouse.gov/about-the-white-house/presidents/franklin-d-roosevelt/#:~:text=Assuming%20the%20Presidency%20at%20the,to%20fear%20is%20fear%20itself.%E2%80%9D
103. Courage is being scared to death but saddling up anyway. (n.d.). Goodreads. Retrieved June 22, 2024, from https://www.goodreads.com/quotes/13533-courage-is-being-scared-to-death-but-saddling-up-anyway
104. American Psychological Association. (n.d.). Building your resilience. American Psychological Association. https://www.apa.org/topics/resilience/building-your-resilience
105. Suzuki, W., with Fitzpatrick, B. (2021). *Good anxiety: Harnessing the power of the most misunderstood emotion.* Atria Books.
106. *Grit: The true story of Steve Young.* (n.d.). YouTube. https://www.youtube.com/watch?v=UYBVSqb2qCw
107. Young, S. (2016). *My life behind the spiral.* Houghton Mifflin Harcourt. 49
108. Steve Young. (n.d.). Wikipedia. Retrieved May 1, 2024, from https://en.wikipedia.org/wiki/Steve_Young
109. Suzuki. (2023). 77.
110. Riordan, H. (2022, October 25). Humans with anxiety are so much braver than they realize. Collective World. https://collective.world/humans-with-anxiety-are-so-much-braver-than-they-realize/
111. Tye, K. (2016, February 2). 7 ways anxiety actually works to your advantage. Good Therapy. https://www.goodtherapy.org/blog/7-ways-anxiety-actually-works-to-your-advantage-0202165
112. 7 surprising ways anxiety benefits you. (2021, November 8). Amen Clinics. https://www.amenclinics.com/blog/7-surprising-ways-anxiety-benefits-you/
113. Rosmarin, D. H. (2023). *Thriving with anxiety: 9 tools to make your anxiety work for you.* Harper Horizon.
114. Rosmarin, D. H. (2023, October 18). 3 ways anxiety can actually help you. *Time Magazine.* https://time.com/6324845/anxiety-beneficial-essay/
115. Suzuki. (2023). 58–59.

ENDNOTES

116. American Psychological Association. (2020, February 1). Building your resilience. American Psychological Association. https://www.apa.org/topics/resilience/building-your-resilience
117. Aristotle. (n.d.). Goodreads. Retrieved July 13, 2024, from https://www.goodreads.com/quotes/7978897-we-are-what-we-repeatedly-do-excellence-then-is-not
118. Clark, D. A. (2013). Cognitive restructuring. In *The Wiley handbook of cognitive behavioral therapy*. Wiley. https://doi.org/10.1002/9781118528563.wbcbt02 . 1–22.
119. Morin, A. L. (2023, May 10). How cognitive reframing works. *Verywell Mind*. https://www.verywellmind.com/reframing-defined-2610419#toc-benefits-of-cognitive-reframing
120. Gillihan, S. (2024, January 11). Cognitive reframing: How it works, what it helps, and more. EverydayHealth.com. https://www.everydayhealth.com/stress/study-says-heres-how-to-reframe-stress-to-use-it-to-your-advantage/
121. Quinn, D. (2023, February 28). Cognitive restructuring in CBT: Steps, techniques, & examples. Sandstone Care. https://www.sandstonecare.com/blog/cognitive-restructuring-cbt/
122. Quinn, D. (2023)
123. Tseng, J., & Poppenk, J. (2020). Brain meta-state transitions demarcate thoughts across task contexts exposing the mental noise of trait neuroticism. *Nature Communications, 11(1)*. https://doi.org/10.1038/s41467-020-17255-9
124. Neuroplasticity. (n.d.). Physiopedia. https://www.physio-pedia.com/Neuroplasticity#:~:text=Neuroplasticity%20refers%20to%20the%20lifelong,between%20neurons%20throughout%20a%20lifetime
125. Facts & statistics: Anxiety and Depression Association of America, ADAA. (n.d.). Anxiety and Depression Association of America (ADAA). https://adaa.org/understanding-anxiety/facts-statistics#:~:text=%2D%20GAD%20affects%206.8%20million%20adults,co%2Doccurs%20with%20major%20depression
126. World Health Organization. (n.d.). COVID-19 pandemic triggers 25% increase in prevalence of anxiety and depression worldwide. World Health Organization. https://www.who.int/news/item/02-03-2022-covid-19-pandemic-triggers-25-increase-in-prevalence-of-anxiety-and-depression-worldwide#:~:text=In%20the%20first%20year%20of,Health%20Organization%20(WHO)%20today
127. Dennis-Tiwary, T. (2022, October 19). How to use anxiety to your advantage. BBC News. https://www.bbc.com/future/article/20221017-how-to-use-anxiety-to-your-advantage
128. Suzuki, W., & Fitzpatrick, B. (2021). 9
129. Carnegie, D. (1944). *How to stop worrying and start living*. Simon & Schuster.
130. Asay, T. P., & Ogletree, M. D. (2022). *Finding peace in difficult times*. Cedar Fort, Inc. 202
131. Just a little inconvenience. (n.d.). Wikipedia. Retrieved July 23, 2024, from https://en.wikipedia.org/wiki/Just_a_Little_Inconvenience
132. Brett, R. (n.d.). If we all threw our problems in a pile. Goodreads. Retrieved July 23, 2024, from https://www.goodreads.com/quotes/127360-if-we-all-threw-our-problems-in-a-pile-and#:~:text=Quote%20by%20Regina%20Brett%3A%20%E2%80%9CIf,pile%20and%20saw%20...%E2%80%9D
133. Adapted from a statement by President Harold B. Lee, Church News, 5 May 1973, 3
134. Lemie Beckner, V. (2023, October 2).

ABOUT THE AUTHORS

Mark D. Ogletree is a professor at Brigham Young University, where he teaches classes on marriage and family relationships. He is also a therapist and has been practicing for the past 35 years. Mark has a bachelor's degree from Brigham Young University in human resource development, a master's degree from Northern Arizona University in mental health counseling, and a Ph.D. from Utah State University in family and human development.

Mark is the author of numerous books and articles on topics ranging from marriage, family, parenting, mental health, and contemporary Church history. His most recent books include *Heaven is Cheering You On, The Making of a Man: A Guide to Raising Strong, Resilient Sons, Beyond the Honeymoon: 25 Questions and Answers about Marital Intimacy,* and *So You're in Love, Now What?*.

Mark has also presented at workshops and academic conferences both nationally and internationally. He and his wife, Janie, reside in Utah. They host a weekly podcast called *Preserving Families*, where they share ideas, principles, and practices to help strengthen families. Mark also hosts another podcast called *Stand by My Servants*, where he discusses with expert scholars the lives and teachings of Apostles and Prophets.

Mark and Janie are also the parents of eight children and 29 grandchildren.

Brayden McFadden is a master's candidate in international affairs at Texas A&M University, specializing in intelligence and defense policy. Before pursuing his graduate studies, he worked as a global threat intelligence analyst and as an operational support technician for the FBI. He holds a bachelor's degree in political science from Brigham Young University, with an emphasis in international strategy and diplomacy and dual minors in history and anthropology.

Brayden has been featured on multiple podcasts and interviews, sharing his experiences as an early-return missionary and discussing the impact of anxiety on his life. This collaboration with Dr. Ogletree marks his first publication, exploring how anxiety can be reframed as a strength.

A Texas native, Brayden grew up playing football, enjoying barbecue, and maintaining a love-hate relationship with the Dallas Cowboys. As the oldest of five children, he has witnessed firsthand the effects of anxiety on those around him. He currently resides in Texas.